Rewriting Germany from the Margins
"Other" German Literature of the 1980s and 1990s

The "margins" in Petra Fachinger's work are occupied largely by second-generation migrant writers from Italy, Spain, and Turkey, German Jowish writers of diverse ethnic origins, and writers born in the GDR. She demonstrates that during the 1980s and 1990s writers from various cultural backgrounds engaged in oppositional discourse to construct their own version of Germany and write back to the German canon. While most studies of texts by minority writers in Germany favour content over form, Fachinger focuses on identifying counter-discursive strategies, and applies postcolonial theory concerned with textual resistance to the German situation. In doing so, this study effectively relates marginal writing in Germany to similar forms of writing in other national and cultural contexts.

The oppositional impulse, whether manifested in counter-canonical discourse, postcolonial picaresque, hybridity, rewriting of genre, or grotesque realism, is prompted by the exclusionary politics of the dominant culture. The discursive strategies used by the authors discussed to rewrite Germany expose the assumptions that underlie German public discourse and destabilize notions of Germanness, Jewishness, and Turkishness. Fachinger's reading of texts by marginal writers in Germany, all of whom endeavour to resist marginalization while simultaneously experiencing or even celebrating the margin as a site of empowerment, was motivated by the absence of comparative studies of such writing. *Rewriting Germany from the Margins* demonstrates the necessity and usefulness of comparative approaches to minority discourses across national and cultural borders.

PETRA FACHINGER is assistant professor in the Department of German Language and Literature, Queen's University.

Rewriting Germany from the Margins

"Other" German Literature of the 1980s and 1990s

PETRA FACHINGER

McGill-Queen's University Press
Montreal & Kingston · London · Ithaca

© McGill-Queen's University Press 2001
ISBN 0-7735-2250-6

Legal deposit fourth quarter 2001
Bibliothèque nationale du Québec

Printed in Canada on acid-free paper

This book has been published with the help of a
grant from the Humanities and Social Sciences
Federation of Canada, using funds provided
by the Social Sciences and Humanities Research
Council of Canada.

McGill-Queen's University Press acknowledges
the financial support of the Government of Canada
through the Book Publishing Industry Development
Program (BPIDP) for its activities. It also
acknowleges the support of the Canada Council
for the Arts for its publishing program.

**National Library of Canada Cataloguing
in Publication Data**

Fachinger, Petra, 1958–
    Rewriting Germany from the margins: "other"
German literature of the 1980s and 1990s
    Includes bibliographical references and index.
    ISBN 0-7735-2250-6
    1. German literature – Minority authors – History
and criticism. 2. German literature – 20th century –
History and criticism. I. Title.
    PT405.F32 2001   830.9'8'0904   C2001-900186-x

Typeset in Palatino 10.5/13
by Caractéra inc., Quebec City

For Patrick and Felix

Contents

Acknowledgments

I first encountered critical thinking about German minority writing that went beyond thematic analysis in the pioneering work of Leslie A. Adelson, Jeffrey Peck, Heidrun Suhr, and Arlene Akiko Teraoka. Sneja Gunew's work on migrant writing in Australia, which has provided many scholars in the emergent field with a theoretical framework, first drew me to the study of migrant literature and has inspired me to continue. I would also like to thank the audiences whose responses to oral versions of some of the material presented in this book helped me refine my ideas.

I would like to thank Peter Quartermain for his critical comments on the introduction of this book and Sander L. Gilman for his insightful and constructive reading of chapter 5. My special thanks go to Kari Grimstad for her critical reading of the final draft. I would also like to thank my colleague Audrey Kobayashi for having been a mentor to me during my first years in a new academic environment.

The second chapter, "Rewriting Turkey: Barbara Frischmuth and Hanne Mede-Flock," contains a revised version of an article entitled "Orientalism Reconsidered: Turkey in Barbara Frischmuth's *Das Verschwinden des Schattens in der Sonne* and Hanne Mede-Flock's *Im Schatten der Mondsichel*" which appeared in *Studies in Twentieth Century Literature* 23.2 (1999): 239–54. I wish to thank the editor of *Studies in Twentieth Century Literature* for permission to reprint this essay.

I would also like to thank Kiepenheuer & Witsch in Cologne for permission to reproduce selected poems by Zehra Çirak from *Fremde Flügel auf eigener Schulter* (1994) and *Vogel auf dem Rücken eines Elefanten* (1991). I am also grateful to Das Arabische Buch for having allowed me to reproduce selected poetry by José F.A. Oliver from various publications.

Preface

When I was teaching an undergraduate survey of German cultural history for the first time in my academic career, I realized that not only had I forgotten much of the pre-twentieth-century German history that I had learned in high school, but that the task of teaching "German culture" was even more daunting. Fortunately, most textbooks do a fairly good job of providing chronological overviews of the most important dates, events, and names from official history, but I found that as the class progressed, students became more interested in the kind of historical information about Germany that was not to be found in the book. What, for example, motivated the young Ferdinand Cohen-Blind to shoot Otto von Bismarck, and what happened to him after the assassination had failed? What do we know about Martin Luther's wife, Katharina von Bora? Where, by the way, are all the women in German history textbooks? Why is there a club of "mixed Germans" in Lomé, Togo? And so on.

The German-born instructor teaching courses in German culture and history is often taken by students to be an expert with "authentic" access to German culture. Not only does this assumption ignore the fact that someone who was born in Germany might know little about other German-speaking countries, but it also ignores the fact that Germany is, culturally speaking, just as divided by regionalism as Canada. Split loyalties add to my dilemma. As someone who has lived in Canada for almost fifteen years, has adopted Canadian citizenship and has consequently forfeited her German/EU passport, I found myself second guessing my use of pronouns: "In Germany, *we*" versus "in Germany, *they*." At other times, I realized that my position as an ex-German living in Canada enables me to view the German cultural scene much more dispassionately. I am able to discuss Germany with cultural distance as well as compare and contrast two national cultures with which I have had prolonged contact.

I am making this point here to draw attention to the problematic nature of "German(y)" and "margin(s)" in the title of this book: *Rewriting Germany from the Margins*. The growing diversity of German culture and literature makes traditional approaches to contemporary German writing inadequate. The question that needs to be addressed is how one can read this literature through a pluralistic and cross-cultural framework without obscuring the specificities of particular cultural situations. A pluralistic approach needs to be fundamentally comparative. I therefore not only compare and contrast "marginal" writing in Germany with "marginal" writing in Canada, the United States, and Australia, but I also emphasize similarities across ethnic and cultural borders without either glossing over the differences or losing sight of dominant, as opposed to "marginal" writing. What the writers to whom I refer as "marginal" have in common is that they share an oppositional and counterdiscursive impulse through which they express the possibility of a community different from that offered by the dominant culture. Such resistance manifests itself in a process of deconstructing the binary structure of centre and margin, rather than replacing the centre. Rewriting thus entails a constructive moment that stresses the importance of agency, and may even anticipate solutions to potential cultural conflicts.

Rewriting nevertheless presupposes that an officially accepted version of the "script" does exist. By implying that the writers discussed in this book "rewrite" German public discourse, I want to emphasize the fact that Germany is a cultural construct. Each of the texts that I analyse renders its own version of Germany and the Germans, just as I myself have been rewriting Germany not only in teaching German cultural history, but also in writing this book.

Rewriting Germany from the Margins

Introduction

While much recent Canadian, American, and Australian criticism has been concerned with rewriting and rereading strategies in ethnic-minority writing, with the exception of Arlene Akiko Teraoka's "*Gastarbeiterliteratur*: The Other Speaks Back," no critical work has yet directly addressed oppositionality in ethnic-minority writing in Germany. This oppositional impulse, however, could well be expected to be especially forceful in a country where "Germanness" was constructed in ethnic terms. Up until 1 January 2000, German citizenship was determined by blood, and national identity was defined by common culture and history. The law denied citizenship to those who had come to Germany as so-called guest workers, as well as to their children and grandchildren, even if they were born in Germany. The guest-worker period, which began in 1955 with the Federal Republic's recruitment contracts with Italy and contracts with Spain in 1960 and Turkey in 1961, ended in 1973 with the termination of labour recruitment ["Anwerbestopp"] during the global economic crisis. Foreign workers were left with the choice of either going back to their countries of origin without a chance of returning to work in Germany later – unless these countries were members of the EEC – or of staying and having their spouses and children move to Germany. However, this measure was not an incentive for workers to return home. It signalled to the guest workers that the time of rotation of labour was over – work contracts prescribed that the workers had to leave after a set number of years to be replaced by new recruits – and the majority opted for family reunification.[1] The shift from transitional stay to long-term residence had taken place.[2] According to the new citizenship law, children born in Germany to non-German parents, one of whom has lived in Germany for at least eight years, receive dual citizenship. Between the ages of eighteen and twenty-three they have to choose whether to keep their German citizenship or that of their parents' country of birth. Immigrants will need to have been in Germany only eight years, instead of the previous fifteen, to be eligible to apply for a German passport. Because of the belatedness of the citizenship reform, Klaus Bade refers to the 1980s – the same case can be made for the 1990s – as a "lost decade,"[3] a decade in which the Federal Republic of Germany evolved into a multicultural country without granting citizenship rights to a large segment of the population.

Furthermore, the rapid shift in 1989 from the East Germans' demand for recognition – "We are *the* people" – to their call for unity with the West – "We are *one* people" – which resulted in the dissolution of the German Democratic Republic, has reframed the question of what it means to be German. Meanwhile, Jews who live in Germany are still officially referred to as cocitizens ["Mitbürger"], and many of them still hesitate to carry a German passport. As Germanness is perceived to be an exclusive quality, opposing notions of West German and foreigner/Jew/East German continue to be propagated in a variety of cultural discourses. Thus questions such as, "how can one be a Jew and a German, a Turk and a German, a Muslim and a German, 'black' and German at the same time?" remain relevant in the construction of German identity.

Construction of German identity became even more complex with the unification of the two German states on 3 October 1990. While former GDR citizens are still struggling to establish themselves within the new Germany, many German Jews[4] feel threatened by Germany's influence within Europe, and ethnic minorities are frustrated by the fact that their opinions about the political process are not given consideration.[5] Unification issues shifted attention away from the so-called foreigner debate, including discussion of the recognition of dual citizenship, and fuelled an increasingly virulent hostility toward ethnic minorities,[6] particularly the Turks.[7] This in turn has motivated these minorities "to return to their roots."[8]

The writers whose texts I discuss in this book are second-generation migrants from Italy, Spain, and Turkey,[9] German Jewish writers of diverse ethnic origins[10] born after World War II, second-generation GDR writers, as well as other contemporary writers who have been marginalized. All of their texts, which were written during the 1980s and 1990s, share an oppositional and counterdiscursive impulse through which they express the possibility of a community different from that offered by the dominant culture. [11] As Arlene Teraoka puts it: "when the silent Turk begins to speak in the dominant language, we can ask to what extent his words represent a collective and oppositional consciousness."[12]

The examination of oppositional discourse has its theoretical foundation in postcolonial criticism concerned with anticolonialist textual resistance.[13] The Australian critic Helen Tiffin, for example, includes within the broad field of the counterdiscursive magic realism, postcolonial picaresque, and allegory, along with "canonical counterdiscourse," the rewriting of a specific text of the canon.[14] I apply the methodology developed by Australian and Canadian critics to the German situation without, however, undervaluing national and cultural specificities. I analyse counterdiscursive modes, such as the rewriting of a specific canonical text [chapters 1, 2, 6, and 7], the rewriting of a traditional genre [chapters 1, 4, 5, and 6], the rewriting of language [particularly chapter 3], postcolonial picaresque [chapter 2], and grotesque realism – see Tiffin's "magic realism" – [chapter 7] within the German context.

In discussing the specific oppositional aesthetics[15] of each text, I pay attention to the particular sociohistorical context of each minority culture and its distinct reaction against German culture, since oppositionality is present in the literary text as a structure of intentionality as much as it is grounded in multiple structures of ideological subject formation. The writers' ethnic background, gender, age, and generation affect the conceptualization of their texts and their choice of oppositional narrative/poetic strategies in significant ways. As I demonstrate in chapters 2, 3, and 5, each of which compares and contrasts the texts of a female and a male writer, these writers' oppositional strategies certainly differ. However, the differences are not shaped exclusively by gender, but also by the other factors listed above.

Russell Ferguson points out in his introduction to *Out There: Marginalization and Contemporary Cultures* that "when we say marginal, we must always ask, marginal to what?"[16] Literature written by those on the margins is usually excluded from the canon or gains entry to it only gradually. In their role of forming a national literature, canonical texts represent a version of that nation's imagined identity and national community. As the canon is a product of choice, that is, a choice of the educated elite and those marketing literature, the process of canon formation and literary evaluation involves power struggles and political conflict. The exclusion of "marginal" texts from the canon is signalled by limited access to publishing houses and by nonconsideration for literary prizes and awards. Thus, it was not until 1991 that for the first time a migrant[17] writer, namely Turkish-born Emine Sevgi Özdamar, received a literary prize other than those – such as the Adelbert von Chamisso Prize – "reserved" for writers who were not born in Germany. Yet, the award of the prestigious Ingeborg Bachmann Prize was not acknowledged at the time in the literature section of *Der Spiegel*, a weekly magazine known for its thorough investigative journalism and critical articles. Furthermore, the *Frankfurter Allgemeine* called the jury's choice a grave error in judgement, describing Özdamar's novel as naïve and folkloristic.[18]

In *Atlas des tropischen Deutschland*, Zafer Şenocak bemoans the German media's general lack of interest in migrant literature and their condescending attitude toward its literary achievements. Jusuf Naoum reinforces Şenocak's assessment when he points out that a book written by a German author about ethnic minorities in Germany is guaranteed to receive lengthy reviews in newspapers and magazines, whereas books written by non-Germans on the same topic are reviewed only collectively, if at all."[19] Furthermore, as Franco Biondi claims in his essay "Die Fremde wohnt in der Sprache" ["Foreignness Lives in Language"] "foreign" writers in Germany are considered to have a weaker command of the German language, and hence less credibility, than their German counterparts. In an attempt to assert his position as a German writer, Biondi states that his objective is "to write against the foreignness in the language."[20] His endeavour therefore becomes a paradoxical one: He makes himself "at home" in the German language by defamiliarizing it and, by playfully breaking its grammatical and syntactical rules, restores and revitalizes it. Similarly, Suleman Taufiq considers counterdiscourse one of the main features of migrant writing in Germany: "We always, almost unintentionally, write against the dominant literary rules and norms of German literature."[21] German critics promptly misread Biondi's subversive rewriting of the German language by drawing attention to faulty sentence structure and unidiomatic expression in reviews of his novel *Abschied der zerschellten Jahre* [*Farewell to the Shattered Years*]. [22]

Apart from branding German migrant writing as inferior in quality, the dominant culture's tendency either to homogenize or to exoticize it contributes further to its ghettoization. As Jusuf Naoum remarks, the German public reduces foreign culture to the "belly dance and kebab."[23] Texts by migrant writers in Germany in the 1970s and early 1980s were usually published in thematic anthologies, the publishers thus implying that migrants from various ethnic backgrounds spoke in a collective voice. The German media also seem to hold fixed notions about the subjects and themes suitable for and relevant to migrant literature, as well as about the migrant's "incorrect" use of standard German. As a result, texts that do not support these stereotypical views are published infrequently, usually by small presses, or not at all. Jusuf Naoum, for example, reports that a colleague's script for a radio play was rejected with the comment: "Guest workers do not talk like this."[24]

Although all migrant writing in Germany is stigmatized in this way, the Turks remain the ethnic minority subjected to the most pervasive and persistent stereotyping. The article in *Der Spiegel* covering the firebomb murder of eight German Turks in Mölln in 1992 and in Solingen in 1993 characterizes German Turks as "icons of foreignness – they are the essential other."[25] And as David Horrocks and Eva Kolinsky put it: "Among the 'others' living in Germany, Turks seem to appear particularly monochrome, culturally backward, an underclass brainwashed by Islamic fundamentalism."[26] Paradoxically, this status as the "essential other," which makes them a prime target of xenophobia and hate crimes, has also come to endow them with a cultural bonus. German publishers tend to reject manuscripts by migrant

writers whose ethnic background is not Turkish with the explanation that cultural institutions subsidize Turkish submissions
only. Iranian-born writer Torkan, for example, complains in an
interview with Leslie Adelson that "foreigners' concerns are automatically assumed to be 'Turkish' concerns."[27] Such apparent
acceptance of German Turkish writing, by equating "the other"
with "the Turk" and at the same time homogenizing "Turks,"
marginalizes it. But, once again, one must ask "marginal" to
what? Other minorities feel that they are pitted against Turks in
competition for government subsidies, while the culture industry
automatically treats all Turkish writers as part of a Turkish subculture. As Aysel Özakin observes, reviews of her works hardly
ever address aesthetic concerns but are always interested in her
status as an "anomalous Turk" ["Ausnahmetürkin"], a status that
she earned because of her intellectual and cosmopolitan views
and life style.[28]

The four Turkish writers whose texts I discuss in this book, Zehra
Çirak, Renan Demirkan, Akif Pirinçci, and Feridun Zaimoglu, were
all born between 1955 and 1964 and grew up in Germany. Their
texts express the second generation's dilemma: they neither have
strong ties to their parents' culture nor are they accepted as Germans or German writers. The discursive strategies and themes in
the texts of this generation of Turkish writers therefore differ from
those of their first-generation colleagues like Güney Dal, Sinasi
Dikmen, Aysel Özakin, Emine Sevgi Özdamar, Aras Ören, and
Yüksel Pazarkaya. Zehra Çirak's poetry, which I discuss in a chapter together with the poetry of José F.A. Oliver, Germany's most
notable writer of Spanish descent, subversively abrogates the "centrality" of the German language and inscribes cultural difference.
These two authors employ a variety of the textual strategies, such
as allusion, code-switching, interlanguage, and syntactic fusion,
identified by the authors of *The Empire Writes Back: Theory and Practice in Post-Colonial Literatures* as characteristic of postcolonial discourses. Here, as in other chapters, I discuss texts by two writers
with significantly different ethnic backgrounds, personal histories,
and cultural positions to underline the importance of reading texts
"beyond ethnicity"[29] without, however, ignoring the differences in
their conceptualization.

Like Zehra Çirak in her poetry, Renan Demirkan in her novel
Schwarzer Tee mit drei Stück Zucker [*Black Tea with Three Lumps of*

Sugar] celebrates cultural hybridity in resisting static notions of authenticity. For her daughter, to whom she is about to give birth, Demirkan's narrator envisions life in a hybrid culture, in which questions of origin and nationality become irrelevant. Demirkan's text also emphasizes the multidimensionality that has shaped her characters prior to arriving in Germany and thus deconstructs the stereotypical image of the Turk as uneducated, fundamentalist, non-European, and unwilling to integrate. With a female narrator who has learned to "talk back,"[30] Demirkan also breaks with the convention of portraying Turkish women as unable to liberate themselves from patriarchal oppression and male dominance.

Hybridity, creolization, and métissage, terms used in postcolonial theory to refer to cultural ambiguity and derived from models developed by writers such as Derek Walcott and E.K. Brathwaite for the literature of the West Indies, are useful within the German context, if one keeps the specificity of each ethnic group's particular position in mind. Women writers of Turkish and Jewish descent, in particular, embrace cultural and national ambiguity as a strategy to redefine their identity. The notion of hybridity is also celebrated within border literature, a term applied mostly to Chicana writing. The border is the trope of difference and the potential conflict between races, cultures, nationalities, class, genders, and sexual orientations. Chicana writer and critic Gloria Anzaldúa in *Borderlands/La Frontera*, for example, gives voice to the new mestiza who celebrates the fragmented physical, national, and cultural experience of the mestiza consciousness and lives in the spaces between the different worlds that she inhabits. In Anzaldúa's utopian view of border culture, national identity, along with other identities, becomes ambiguous and will ultimately lose its segregating power in favour of a culture of *mestizaje* and hybridization.[31] In like manner, border writing becomes a site of subversion through intertextuality and the mixing of genres and language.

Feridun Zaimoglu, author of the three provocative texts *Kanak Sprak* [*Kanak Language*], *Abschaum* [*Scum*], and *Koppstoff* [*Head Stuff*], all published by Rotbuch Verlag, a publishing company that specializes in cultural studies and texts by writers who are critical of the mainstream, takes a different position. His texts, which can be compared to the street ethnography of African American rappers, portray the outlaw culture of the *Kanaksta*.[32] In

Zaimoglu's opinion, the identity crisis of German Turks is a myth created by social workers. Consequently, hybridization as Çirak and Demirkan envision it, is pointless to him. In a language to which he refers as *Kanak Sprak* and which he describes as a creole or thieves' slang with secret codes and signs and with a style that can best be identified as grotesque realism, Zaimoglu positions the culture of the *Kanaksta* at the margins of society. Just as rappers hyperbolize the media image of "lawless black youth," Zaimoglu exaggerates the media image of the "Turk" to undermine it until the *Kanaksta* becomes exactly what "Germans" fear.

Zaimoglu also targets Günter Wallraff's undercover reportage *Ganz Unten* [*At the Bottom*], which has significantly contributed to the reification of the "Turk" as the "essential Other" and "icon of foreignness." Partly because of its legal repercussions, which received an inordinate amount of media attention, this text has greatly influenced public opinion of and public discourse about Turks in Germany. In his books, Zaimoglu satirizes Wallraff's claims that the "Turk" is at the bottom, that the "Turk" is unable to speak idiomatically and grammatically correct German, and that the "Turk" is unable to voice opposition to oppression and exploitation. Another second-generation Turkish writer, Akif Pirinçci, who published his first book in 1980, paved the way for Zaimoglu's street ethnography by making a clear break with the social realism of "guest-worker literature."

Of the four Turkish writers whose texts I discuss in this book, Akif Pirinçci is the one who most adamantly refuses to be identified with the margin. His best-selling novel *Felidae*, a crime novel about cats that has also been made into a film, *Der Rumpf* [*Torso*], a novel about a man with no arms and legs, who commits the "perfect" murder, and his most recent novel *Yin* have no subject matter that might link them with ethnic-minority writing. Ironically, despite his commercial success, his insistence that he is not an ethnic writer, has doubly marginalized him culturally. His texts are discussed neither in books on migrant writing nor in books on mainstream German literature. His first novel, *Tränen sind immer das Ende* [*Tears Are Always the End*], a semiautobiographical account of a young German Turk's unhappy love story with a young German woman, met with the same fate.

Juxtaposing Akif Pirinçci's *Tränen sind immer das Ende* with Franco Biondi's *Abschied der zerschellten Jahre*, I demonstrate how these two writers adopt "canonical counterdiscourse"[33] to write back to the German "masters." While Biondi's *Abschied der zerschellten Jahre* can be read as a rewriting both of the *Novelle*, the German "national genre," and of Gottfried Keller's *Romeo and Julia auf dem Dorfe* [*Romeo and Julia in the Village*], Pirinçci uses GDR writer Ulrich Plenzdorf's *Die neuen Leiden des jungen W.* [*The New Sorrows of Young W.*], itself a rewriting of Goethe's *Die Leiden des jungen Werthers* [*The Sorrows of Young Werther*], as a model for his *Tränen sind immer das Ende* in order to define his own text's relationship to the German canon.

Tränen sind immer das Ende also holds a key position within migrant writing in German as it was the first text to refuse to adopt the authentic and realistic discursive practices of migrant literature prevalent at the time of its publication. This discourse was promulgated by Franco Biondi, Jusuf Naoum, Rafik Schami, and Suleman Taufiq, the founding members of the Polynationale Literatur- und Kunstverein. Akif Pirinçci wrote his novel at a time when analogies between increasing hostility towards Turks and anti-Semitism in Nazi Germany were frequently drawn in public discourse.[34] By repeatedly, apparently innocently, alluding to concentration camp atrocities in his text, Pirinçci demonstrates how language can be abused and to what extent the German past is still haunting its language. Besides drawing an analogy between the German response to the Turkish presence in contemporary Germany and the German response to the Jewish presence in the Third Reich, Pirinçci also establishes a cultural link between the "foreign other" in West Germany and the "East German other." By rewriting Goethe's text through East German writer Ulrich Plenzdorf's text, Pirinçci draws attention to positional similarities between the literature of the GDR (a literature that has always had the dubious status of other within the "German" canon) and literature by so-called foreigners.

With unification, the construction of the "other" within the discourse in the west of Germany has undergone a curious modification. As Nora Räthzel points out, "the arrival of ethnic Germans [the majority of whom come from the former Soviet Union, Poland, and Rumania] in large numbers first contradicted the stereotype that all Germans were German-speaking people, socialised by a western capitalist lifestyle."[35] East Germans, according to Räthzel, "at first seemed to offer a solution: now a distinction could be made between the ethnic Germans and 'real Germans' who spoke the language and came from a country that, in spite of political differences, has always claimed itself as German."[36] However, over the last few years, East Germans "have lost their Germanness and become the other," stereotyped by West Germans as inefficient, old-fashioned, unqualified, and authoritarian. According to Räthzel, "all these negative characteristics, however, have to do not with their being 'German by blood,' but with their being socialised by the Communist system. East Germans are considered as socially and culturally different, not different by nature."[37] Andreas Huyssen speaks of a "wholesale rejection of GDR culture, which was taken to be as polluted as Bitterfeld/Leuna, as obsolete by Western standards as the steel conglomerate of Eisenhüttenstadt, as bloated as any old collective farm."[38] Furthermore, as he points out, the defamation of GDR culture went hand in hand with "the demand for a reassessment of the role intellectuals and writers had played in the 40 year [sic] history of the Federal Republic."[39]

Kerstin Jentzsch and Thomas Brussig are two young writers born in the GDR who satirize the unification process, the corruption of that state's political system, as well as life in the free-market society. Their novels demonstrate the use of strategies that can best be described as postcolonial picaresque. While the unified Germany has officially been a "postcolonial" nation since it was granted full sovereignty by the occupying powers, German unification is often perceived as an act of Western colonization of the East. In *Seit die Götter ratlos sind* [*Since the Gods Haven't a Clue*], Kerstin Jentzsch writes back to Christa Wolf's narrative *Kassandra* and to *Voraussetzungen einer Erzählung: Kassandra* [*Preconditions of a Narrative: Cassandra*], a text that contextualizes and theorizes Wolf's narrative. As Andreas Huyssen claims, writers such as Christa Wolf and Heiner Müller, whose texts were celebrated in the GDR and the FRG as major achievements, had been given the dissident bonus while actual dissidents, mostly of the younger generation, were "harrassed [sic], jailed, expelled, or 'eased out' of the GDR."[40] With the creation of her *pícara*, an enthusiastic, unprejudiced traveller who lives in the present and enjoys life, Jentzsch criticizes as life-denying the GDR predilection for the classical past as celebrated in both the texts of its most respected writers and in school curricula. Likewise, Thomas Brussig's anti-hero blames his parents' generation and Christa Wolf, whom he accuses by proxy for all the GDR writers of her generation, for what he perceives as their strategic silence and lack of resistance. In *Helden wie wir* [*Heroes Like Us*], Brussig rewrites Wolf's controversial narrative *Was bleibt* [*What Remains*], which records a day in the life of a woman writer under surveillance by the State Security Service in March 1979, from the perspective of one of the young Stasi agents spying on Wolf's first-person narrator. Both Jentzsch and Brussig also parody certain colonial linguistic phenomena peculiar to GDR German that mainly served purposes of propaganda and indoctrination. The picaresque, a literary genre that was not in favour in the society in which Jentzsch and Brussig grew up because of its critical and subversive potential, the alienation of its protagonist from society, and, in some cases, its erotic overtones, turns out to be an appropriate genre to express the ambivalent feelings about unification that the two authors voice through their protagonists.

Unification has also radically altered the way in which Jewish writers in Germany have come to construct their identity. With the fall of the Berlin Wall, as Sander Gilman claims,[41] the Holocaust became the obsolete past, and the demise of the GDR constituted the "new past." Unlike Jurek Becker and Edgar Hilsenrath, two "established" Jewish authors, born in 1937 and 1926 respectively, young Jewish writers in Germany, that is, those born in the late 1950s and in the 1960s, do not write about the Holocaust. As Elena Lappin explains in the introduction to *Jewish Voices, German Words: Growing Up Jewish in Postwar Germany and Austria*, "these authors cannot, in any straightforward sense, be considered heirs to a continuous German-Jewish literary tradition. They can no longer assimilate into the German literary environment, 'passing,' as could their predecessors, for German authors."[42] My discussion of the autobiographies of two German Jewish writers demonstrates how the relationship between Jews and Germans constitutes a crucial part in any construction of both German and German Jewish identity. According to Jack Zipes, who observes a growing "German fascination for things Jewish," the resurgence of Jewish culture in Germany "has compelled the attention of Germans during the past fifteen years and altered their views of Jewishness and themselves."[43] He also expresses the hope that this development may have "laid the groundwork for a different kind of relationship, not dominated by guilt and certainly opposed to the anti-Semitism and xenophobia exhibited by a small minority of Germans today."[44] In his view, the rise of German nationalism and Jewish consciousness are closely related and "Germans and Jews have never been as active and concerned in the post-Auschwitz era to identify themselves via the other as they have been"[45] during the 1980s and 1990s.

Lea Fleischmann in *Dies ist nicht mein Land: Eine Jüdin verläßt die Bundesrepublik* [*This Is Not My Land: A Jewish Woman Leaves Germany*] and Richard Chaim Schneider in *Zwischen Welten: Ein jüdisches Leben im heutigen Deutschland* [*Between Worlds: A Jewish Life in Germany Today*] both resort to essayistic writing[46] within these autobiographies to give their voices more critical and political weight. Their portrayal of personal experience thus becomes an analysis of German Jewish life in Germany, the relationship between Germans and Jews in contemporary Germany, and German ways of dealing with the Holocaust. Although many contemporary autobiographies do not conform to the generally accepted rules of autobiographical writing, this has not been so within the context of German Jewish autobiography. Fleischmann and Schneider, on the other hand, break new ground by selfconsciously subverting autobiographical conventions. Fleischmann rewrites the conventional structure of Holocaust autobiography [life before camp, initiation into and endurance of camp life, and escape from the camp][47] with a twist. While Holocaust autobiographies often begin with a description of the place where the survivor/narrator grew up, focusing on the spiritual and religious strength of his or her community in the face of adversity, the part in Fleischmann's own autobiography corresponding to life before camp relates her childhood experiences in a German camp for displaced persons where she was cut off from Jewish spirituality and tradition. This description of her early life is followed by an account of her initiation into and endurance of the German education system as a teacher. She finally escapes a life she perceives as defined by rules and restrictions by emigrating to Israel. Fleischmann, in her analysis of German life and education, points out how important it was for her to unlearn conformism and to acquire oppositional strategies to be able to survive.

Richard Chaim Schneider, on the other hand, who is ten years younger than Fleischmann, emphasizes the importance for each generation of German Jews of redefining their relationship with Germans as well as their own identity as German Jews. He also points out how volatile life in the German Jewish Diaspora is and to what extent it is affected by both national and international political events such as the Israeli invasion of Lebanon, the so-called Fassbinder scandal, [48] the Bitburg affair,[49] the German historians' debate,[50] the fall of the Berlin Wall, and peace negotiations in the Middle East. While conventional autobiographies open with the writer's birth and childhood and frequently culminate in some kind of conversion experience, Schneider chooses to begin with the relation of his own conversion experience, triggered by the Fassbinder affair, which transformed him from a German Jew feeling comfortable with the *status quo* to a Jew sensitive to growing anti-Semitism in Germany and wary of worldwide political changes. Both autobiographies can also be read as writing back to the flood of non-Jewish autobiographical texts responding to the Holocaust,[51] a phenomenon that began in the 1960s and peaked after the national telecast of the American television series *Holocaust* in 1979, watched by over twenty million people of the FRG.[52] The film chronicles the lives of two fictional German families – one Jewish, one Nazi – during the Third Reich. The viewer learns about the Nuremberg Laws, the *Kristallnacht*, Buchenwald, Theresienstadt, Babi-Yar, and Auschwitz through the personal lives of the family members. As Anton Kaes points out: "*Holocaust*, the movie, was preceded by an intense information campaign about Holocaust, the event. Government agencies, schools, churches, television and radio stations, newspapers, and magazines were all involved in disseminating information about the Final Solution. The whole country was mobilized and ready to watch the American recounting of a tabooed period of German history."[53]

Like Richard Chaim Schneider, Barbara Honigmann refuses to define *Heimat* geographically. Anat Feinberg demonstrates in "Abiding in a Haunted Land: The Issue of Heimat in Contemporary German-Jewish Writing," how complex issues of *Heimat* are for German Jewish writers. To what degree they will be able to feel at home in Germany is determined by their ethnic background, age, generation, and gender. Honigmann who grew up in the GDR[54] and emigrated to Strasbourg, shows in her "border novel" *Roman von einem Kinde* [*Novel of a Child*][55] how cultural ambiguity, which might be experienced as painful by some, is ultimately liberating and life affirming. Honigmann rewrites the anti-Semitic myth of the wandering Jew[56] who, exiled from home, is condemned to diasporic suffering, by suggesting instead an alternative space and community in the borderlands. Apart from transgressing the boundaries of fiction and autobiography, novel and short story, poetry and fiction, Honigmann's *Roman von einem Kinde*, like Renan Demirkan's *Schwarzer Tee mit drei Stück Zucker*, uses the crossing of national, geographical, religious, and physical borders as a major trope.

If Turkish writers both benefit and suffer from the cultural bonus with which mainstream German society endows them, the ethnic bonus which Germans and the German culture industry confer on German Jews is even more of a burden to German Jewish writers. As Elena Lappin explains, "observed with curiosity as exotic representatives of an almost extinct species, they attract a great deal of critical attention."[57] The fact that their books are widely read and reviewed by Germans makes some German Jewish writers uncomfortable. Esther Dischereit, for example, observes in an interview that writing for a non-Jewish German audience has "a touch of prostitution – Jewish prostitution ... but the alternative would be to be silent."[58] And just as manuscripts by German migrant writers are rejected by German publishers if they do not conform to German expectations of how the migrant speaks, Rafael Seligmann experienced a similar dilemma when attempting to find a publisher for his controversial novel *Rubinsteins Versteigerung* [*Rubinstein's Auction*]. As he explains in *Mit beschränkter Hoffnung: Juden, Deutsche, Israelis* [*With Limited Hope: Jews, Germans, Israelis*], Hoffman & Campe, who had published Lea Fleischmann's autobiography, after initially showing some interest, told him that no Jew talks to his parents in a tone as disrespectful as that of his protagonist Jonathan; they preferred not to expose their readers to that image of German Jews. The paralysing effect of the relationship between Germans and Jews can also be illustrated by the bizarre detour that Edgar Hilsenrath's satirical novel *Der Nazi & der Friseur*, written in 1968, had to take before it appeared in Germany. While the American translation of the novel, *The Nazi and the Barber: A Tale of Vengeance*, was published as early as 1971, it took another six years before the German original appeared in an obscure publishing house.

The chapter "Rewriting Turkey" reverses the gaze by discussing a revisionary reading of Turkey as presented in the novel of a "marginal" West German writer. In her novel *Im Schatten der Mondsichel* [*In the Shadow of the Crescent Moon*], published by the fringe publishing house EXpress Edition, Hanne Mede-Flock writes back to *Das Verschwinden des Schattens in der Sonne* [*The Shadow Disappears in the Sun*][59] by the Austrian writer Barbara Frischmuth. Recent German criticism has demonstrated that the relationships of Germany and Austria with the orient have been more complicated than Edward Said's *Orientalism* makes it appear. Both Frischmuth and Mede-Flock represent the interaction of their female protagonists with the orient as more complex and less "colonizing" than that of the male protagonists' in texts by male twentieth-century German and Austrian writers.

While Barbara Frischmuth rewrites the *Bildungsroman* to subvert Eurocentric assumptions underlying travel literature, Hanne Mede-Flock writes back to Frischmuth by shifting the focus from the individual to the community and from urban to rural Turkey. And whereas Frischmuth's text is an early response to male travel writing about the orient such as Elias Canetti's *Die Stimmen von Marrakesch* [*The Voices of Marrakesh*] (1967), Mede-Flock's text can be read as a response to novels like *Das Verschwinden des Schattens in der Sonne*, which from a feminist point of view might seem apolitical and esoteric. Frischmuth's novel evokes stereotypical images of the protagonist's home country, which the reader has reason to believe is Austria, as a peaceful country that does not provide the need for political action and therefore fails to prepare the protagonist for her stay in Turkey, a country represented as a place haunted by violence. Mede-Flock, on the other hand, depicts the clashes between demonstrators and police at a peace march in Germany as almost equally violent as those in Turkey. By dedicating the novel to Nuriye Bekir, who was stabbed by her husband in front of a women's shelter in Berlin as her four children looked on, Mede-Flock draws attention to the fact that, with the arrival of Turkish migrants in Germany and a growing Turkish German population, Turkey has moved closer to Germany than Germans ever thought possible. This new reality, so the novel suggests, requires that orient and occident learn from each other.

Feridun Zaimoglu, however, as I demonstrate in the final chapter, undermines such liberal discourse.

Margin and centre, regardless of national context, "can draw their meanings only from each other,"[60] and, as postcolonial critics have observed, the margin tends to speak back from the periphery in an attempt to resist and deconstruct the centre. Most importantly, both margin and centre are floating signifiers. They shift their meaning according to how those on the margin define themselves, the centre, and their relationship to each other at a particular historical moment. Thus, all texts discussed in this book project a different image of Germany and the Germans, and their authors construct their marginal position uniquely. Although some of the writers like Franco Biondi, Richard Chaim Schneider, and Zafer Şenocak have assumed the role of spokesperson for both their own and other groups in Germany, others, like Akif Pirinçci and Feridun Zaimoglu, refuse to be identified as minority writers. Others still, like Lea Fleischmann and Barbara Honigmann, consider themselves as selfexiled outsiders.

My reading of texts by "marginal" writers in Germany, who all endeavour to resist marginalization while simultaneously experiencing or even celebrating the margin as a site of empowerment, is motivated by the absence of comparative studies of such writing. Furthermore, most discussions of ethnic-minority writing in Germany lack awareness of ethnic-minority writing in other cultural contexts and of the theoretical approaches to such literature. As Gayatri Spivak observes in *Outside in the Teaching Machine*, "marginal studies" necessarily call for interdisciplinary investigation. By reading "marginal" writing in Germany that positions itself in opposition to the centre through postcolonial theories and theories of ethnic and diasporic writing, this book attempts to demonstrate the necessity and usefulness of comparative approaches to minority discourses across national borders without, however, undervaluing the specificities of the local, the ethnic group, and the nation.

1 Writing Back to Keller and Goethe: Franco Biondi and Akif Pirinçci

In *Decolonising Fictions*, Diana Brydon and Helen Tiffin call the rewriting of European texts by writers from postcolonial societies a "recuperative strategy." They claim that a reconstruction of the colonial text "can only occur as a dynamic interaction between European hegemonic systems and peripheral subversion of them,"[1] that is, "exposing" the assumptions that underlie the dominant discourse and "dis/mantling" them.[2] The two critics conclude that postcolonial literatures should therefore not be regarded as "extensions" of British literature but as "oppositional or counter" to it.[3] In Germany, the relationship between German literature and literature written in German by those not born there or born to non-German parents has been debated now for over two decades. In 1983, one year before Franco Biondi published *Abschied der zerschellten Jahre*, Harald Weinrich, who teaches at the Institute for German as a Foreign Language in Munich, in "Um eine deutsche Literatur von außen bittend" ["A Request for a German Literature from the Outside"] defined German migrant literature as an extension of German literature, referring to migrant writers as "German writers who come from outside."[4] Some of these writers, according to Weinrich, may become "masters" of the German language just like their canonized German colleagues.[5] To prove his point he gives the example of Elias Canetti, who, although he was not born into the German language, was one of its "masters," a fact that was acknowledged by the Bayerische Akademie der Schönen Künste as early as 1969, when it awarded him its literary prize, the same prize awarded to Biondi in 1983. Not only does Weinrich disregard here the particular position of Jewish writers writing in German, but, like Maria Frisé in her review of Franco Biondi's text, from which I quote in the Introduction (note 22), he measures a writer's merits by his or her ability to "master" the German language, whatever that is supposed to mean. Furthermore, by making the explicit distinction between writers who come "from outside" and those who are "on the inside," he contributes to the polarization between those who belong and are eligible to receive literary awards and those who do not belong.

Franco Biondi and Akif Pirinçci adopt narrative strategies comparable to those used by postcolonial authors to write back to the German masters. Franco Biondi,[6] who was one of the major advocates for the rights of guest workers in Germany during the 1970s and 1980s, received the Adelbert von Chamisso Prize in 1987. As Heidrun Suhr points out, "the naming of this prize is another indication of the attitude of these supporters [members of the Institute for German as a Foreign Language in Munich]."[7] In her opinion, the only thing the French count has in common with migrant writers in Germany is the fact that he also wrote in German. Focusing on this similarity, according to Suhr, ignores important differences.[8] While Franco Biondi has always been involved in the debate over the status of migrant writing in Germany, Akif Pirinçci has "purposely put himself beyond the scope of *any* foreigner's literature,"[9] as Marilya Veteto-Conrad describes his position. Like his protagonist Akif in *Tränen sind immer das Ende* (1980), Pirinçci emigrated with his parents from Turkey to Germany at the age of nine. In contrast to the first-generation Turkish German writers Aras Ören and Aysel Özakin, the majority of whose texts were published in German translation in the 1970s and early 1980s, Pirinçci, like all the other second-generation writers discussed in this book, writes exclusively in German.

For migrants from the Mediterranean who, like Franco Biondi, came to Germany as guest workers in the 1960s and 1970s, German is a "language of power" because of Germany's economic hegemony and the individual worker's dependence on a German-speaking government and employer. German is also the lingua franca to which migrants with different mother tongues resort in order to communicate with each other. As Biondi claims in his essay, "Die Fremde wohnt in der Sprache," writing in German does not for him mean writing in a foreign language but writing in "opposition to" the "foreignness" in the language.[10] He uses etymology and morphology to first make himself "at home" in the German language, only to "defamiliarize" it by placing words in unfamiliar contexts and by breaking grammatical rules in an attempt to "recover" meaning. To write against the "foreignness" in the German language can therefore be understood in two ways: either to overcome the "foreignness" by exploring it and adapting to it, or as to oppose and subvert it. In *Abschied der zerschellten Jahre* (1984), Biondi employs "recuperative" [Brydon/Tiffin] and oppositional strategies not only on the micro level of the text, that is, in grammatical structures and idiomatic expressions, but also on the macro level, namely in the structural components of the traditional *Novelle*. By displacing and replacing these components he intends to draw attention to their original function and meaning and also invest them with new meaning.

The *Novelle* is the offspring of one of the earliest literary exchanges between Germany and Italy. The first Germans writing critically about the *Novelle*, Christoph Martin Wieland, the brothers Schlegel, and Ludwig Tieck, cited *Il Decamerone* as one of the first examples of the genre. The history of the *Novelle* in Germany begins with Goethe's *Unterhaltungen deutscher Ausgewanderten* [*Conversations of German Refugees*] – an adaptation of Boccaccio's *Il Decamerone* – in which refugees escaping the turmoil of the French Revolution entertain themselves by telling each other stories about events that brought about significant changes in their lives. In one of his conversations with Eckermann, Goethe defines the *Novelle* as "a true, unprecedented event."[11] Gradually, the German term *Novelle*, taken from the Italian *novella*, in which the etymological meaning *novum* [new, not yet heard of] was obvious, became the label to distinguish the *Novelle* from the "*Roman*," the German word for novel. Like Goethe, Tieck emphasizes the importance of plot over character in the *Novelle*, in contrast to the "*Roman*," and therefore claims the turning point as its most distinguishing feature.

A.D. Harvey maintains that it was not, however, until the second half of the nineteenth century with Paul Heyse's further specification of what distinguishes the *Novelle* from other short prose narratives – for example, its elaborate use of leitmotifs – that the term *Novelle* was established "as the only correct mode of referring to a distinct and unmistakably German genre."[12] Harvey sees the reason for the unique critical and theoretical attention given to the *Novelle* in nineteenth-century Germany in the absence of a novel tradition comparable to that in England, France, and Italy. He concludes: "No great German novelist between Goethe and Theodor Fontane comes to mind: only 'Novelle' writers."[13] In other words, the *Novelle* is as German as the modern short story is American, the long poem Canadian, and the *corridos* Mexican.

By calling *Abschied der zerschellten Jahre* a *Novelle*, Franco Biondi places his text within the German literary tradition. The narrative displays features long associated with the genre i.e., a limited cast of participants, a relatively tight, single plotline, a turning point, and even a Heysian "Falke."[14] His *Novelle* deals with the fate of twenty-year-old Mamo, the son of guest-worker parents who are told by the authorities that the apartment in which they have lived for twenty years is too small for a family of six. Not being able to find an apartment large enough to comply with German regulations,[15] they decide to return to their country of origin, unspecified in the text. The description of the family's dilemma draws attention to the insecure legal status of the guest workers, who even after twenty years of residence had no claim to German citizenship, as well as the Kafkaesque enforcement of the law by the German authorities. When Mamo, who has his residence permit, loses his job, he, too, receives a letter from the immigration office telling him to leave Germany. He, however, decides to stay, since he regards Germany as home. Equipped with a gun, he barricades himself in the apartment waiting for the police and, in the end, apparently shoots one of the officers. The dramatic opening of the *Novelle* is followed by a series of flashbacks, which reveal the hostility of some of the young Germans towards Mamo, the disintegration of his relationship with his girlfriend Dagmar, and his friendship with Costas, the old, blind neighbour.

By beginning his narrative with the turning point, Biondi rewrites the traditional structure of the *Novelle*. The displacement of the turning point suggests that it is not the desperate deed of a young man that should be called "unprecedented" but the "unprecedented," that is inhumane, sociopolitical circumstances that drive Mamo to defend himself with a gun. Biondi not only rewrites certain structural features of the genre but also writes back to one specific *Novelle*: Gottfried Keller's *Romeo und Julia auf dem Dorfe* (1856), which enjoyed an uncontested position not only in German high-school curricula, but also in those of institutions, such as the *Studienkolleg* where "foreigners" make their first contact with German literature.[16]

Keller's *Novelle* is an adaptation of Shakespeare's *Romeo and Juliet*, which, among other things, dramatizes the conflict between individual love and an outdated code of honour. In *Romeo und Julia auf dem Dorfe*, Keller describes the destructive impact of bourgeois greed and fear of difference on an agrarian community. The *Novelle* concludes with the suicide of the young lovers Vrenchen and Sali, whose marriage is made impossible not only by Sali's assault on Vrenchen's father, leaving the latter mentally deranged, but also by Swiss law, which until 1874, prohibited marriage between the homeless.[17] Ironically, the feud between the two families is brought on by the fight over a piece of land to which, as they are well aware, the Black Fiddler is heir. This vagrant outlaw, however, cannot prove his identity and is thus not able to claim the land. If the townspeople of Seldwyla would only let him have his property, he assures them, he will sell it and use the money to emigrate.[18] In both *Romeo und Julia auf dem Dorfe* and *Abschied der zerschellten Jahre*, the bone of contention is space: a contested piece of land and an apartment that the authorities call too small.

Biondi also adopts from his literary predecessors the motif of the two lovers who cannot stay together because society does not approve of their union. When Mamo overcomes his shame sufficiently to be able to discuss the impending deportation with Dagmar, she suggests that they leave together for "his country of origin," a suggestion that proves to him that she, too, regards him as a foreigner and does not understand that Germany is where he belongs. Biondi makes it clear that it is not Dagmar who is to blame, but, just as in *Romeo and Juliet* and *Romeo und Julia auf dem Dorfe*, society and the values and restrictions it imposes on the individual. Like Vrenchen, Dagmar seems to be prepared to commit suicide. The couple's alienation from each other in their final conversation, however, shows that Keller's version of the old story, union in death if not in life, turns into dystopia for an Italian migrant writing in 1984 in the Federal Republic.

In transforming suicide into homicide, Biondi retains Keller's social criticism, writing it into his own time and into his own frame of reference: xenophobia and the government's refusal to reform its citizenship law. Keller ironically paraphrases the newspaper report that inspired him by ending his *Novelle* with the comment that the lovers' suicide was a sign of a spreading moral depravation and the unruliness of passion. Biondi's narrator also apparently withdraws towards the end of the text. He presents the reader with various perspectives on Mamo's shooting of the officer and the events that lead up to it. Keller's irony turns with Biondi into tragedy, when Mamo fires into the crowd while listening to a televised speech by Chancellor Helmut Kohl who encourages guest workers to return home ["Förderung der Rückkehrbereitschaft"] and Germans to be more tolerant.[19] Biondi not only destabilizes his text by leaving the end open and presenting Mamo's fate from different perspectives, but he also shifts the point of view throughout the narrative, thus preventing the reader from feeling comfortable with a familiar narrative site.

Franco Biondi also refuses to give Mamo a specific ethnic identity. When asked about his ethnic background, Mamo answers that he is from no man's land, just like Ulysses who, when confronting the Cyclops, called himself Nobody to save his life: "Besides, I am from no man's land ... just like Ulysses; as is well known, he told the Cyclops that his name was Nobody to save his life. I'm doing the same thing."[20] The text implicitly identifies the uncouth, one-eyed, man-eating giants of Greek mythology with the Germans, and the discriminated against and besieged foreigner with Ulysses. In the *Odyssey*, Ulysses outsmarts Polyphemus by telling him that his ship shattered on the cliffs [hence the adjective "zerschellt" (shattered) in the title of Biondi's text], stranding him and his companions on the island, and by calling himself Nobody in order to prevent other Cyclops from helping Polyphemus, who identifies his enemy to them as Nobody. Mamo's ethnicity is also defined by negation: "He is no Turk," someone points out in his defence. Since Mamo does not identify with his parents' ethnicity, he has no ethnic memory.

The old man Costas, a Tiresias-like figure, serves as a surrogate ethnic memory in the text. Costas, who is a much more positive figure and reliable guide than Friar Laurence and the Black Fiddler, spends most of the day sitting in the courtyard, staring, so it seems to those passing by, at the walls of the apartment building. When Mamo asks what he is doing, Costas answers that he is trying to recover his country's history, a history that was interrupted by mass emigration. In the old times, Costas explains, people would come together to listen to stories. He tells Mamo a story about abuse of power and usurpation, the destruction of his village by an unscrupulous businessman, who deprived the fishing community of its independent economic base. As in Keller's *Novelle*, the advent of industrialization and capitalism proves to have a devastating impact on the agrarian community. Furthermore, Costas's story, which grows out of another culture with a different way of life, disrupts the flow of the narrative dealing with Mamo's fate. It is the other reclaiming its space. Just as the uncultivated strip of land in *Romeo und Julia auf dem Dorfe*, which is eventually reclaimed by weeds and shrubs, lies between the two fields cultivated by the two farmers Manz and Marti, Costas's story is surrounded by "deterritorialized" prose and spills over its boundaries by repeatedly interrupting the main narrative. Costas's voice "reterritorializes," on the textual level, the space that his community has lost. Keller's young lovers cannot live in no man's land, symbolized by the uncultivated strip of land,[21] and Mamo refuses to return to his parents' country, a no man's land to him. Mamo does not kill a Tybalt, nor does he strike at Dagmar's father, whom he has never met. Defending his territory, he kills an official representative of the country that refuses to function as his "fatherland." By denying renewal of a residence permit to Mamo, who was born and raised in Germany and does not speak any language other than German, the authorities also deny him the right to speak his mother tongue. Metaphorically, when Mamo takes aim at the heart of the police officer, he fires at the "heart" of the German language.[22]

The image of the heart functions as a leitmotif – Heyse's *Falke* – in *Abschied der zerschellten Jahre*. The motif appears first when Mamo demonstrates his shooting skills on the fairground, drawn by the specific nature of the target: playing cards with three red hearts. After Mamo wins twice in a row, the gallery owner offers some proverbial wisdom: good marksmen are like lovers; both hit the heart. The heart also establishes a further intertextual link with Keller's *Novelle*. When Keller's lovers spend their last afternoon at the country fair, Vrenchen buys Sali a gingerbread heart, which has a proverb written on each side: "A sweet almond is my love for you!" and "Once you have eaten this heart, don't forget: Much sooner than my love, my brown eyes will fade."[23] While the proverbs in *Romeo und Julia auf dem Dorfe* foreshadow the lovers' suicide, Biondi uses various idiomatic expressions containing the word "heart" in *Abschied der zerschellten Jahre* to reveal the hollowness of a language that relies on clichés and stock responses.

A leitmotif used in a similarly oppositional way to *Herz* is *Spieß* [spear], which invites association with the stake with which Ulysses blinds Polyphemus. At the beginning of the story, when Mamo tries to come to terms with the impending deportation, he blames himself for not having anticipated the turn of events and refers to those who are in power as "calling the shots"[24] and to his gun as his spear. Furthermore, towards the end of the text, imagining what the tabloids will report about the shooting, Mamo concludes: "They already know everything in advance. Nothing is true in this day and age. They always turn the tables on you."[25] Turning the tables is an apt image for Biondi's various strategies of oppositional practice throughout the text, for example, as in his rewriting of the hero's return. Ulysses returns home to Ithaca at the end of the *Odyssey,* and as Hans Wysling has demonstrated, the return home is one of the central motifs in the prose fiction of Gottfried Keller, who called his novel *Der grüne Heinrich* [*Green Henry*] the *Odyssey* of the nineteenth century.[26] Wysling compares the end of *Romeo und Julia auf dem Dorfe*, where Jerusalem is emerging from the river, with the "coming home" of the lovers at the conclusion of the "Song of Solomon."[27] In contrast, Biondi's protagonist is not only alone at the end of *Abschied der zerschellten Jahre,* but he also refuses to return "home." When the police storm the apartment building, using tear gas, Mamo comments: "My apartment has truly become a preliminary heaven."[28] He adds that his father once lectured his children on death and paradise from the very spot in the living room where he is standing now to confront the officers. Biondi makes it clear that the members of the second generation, the children of guest workers born in Germany, are "homeless" in several ways. Not only are they cut off from their parents' "ethnic" heritage, but they are also denied the right to participate in the only culture they know.

In "Die Fremde wohnt in der Sprache," Franco Biondi sees the construction of "foreignness" in the political discourse about "foreigners" reflected in the majority's criticism of the minority's deviation from grammatical rules. According to Biondi, the "foreign" writer in Germany is regarded as having less "power over the German language" and therefore less authority as a writer. Some responses to *Abschied der zerschellten Jahre*, like that of Maria Frisé, confirm Biondi's claim. In these readings of Biondi's text, the reader "dominates the text," as Elizabeth A. Flynn sees it, that is, he or she "resist[s] the alien thought or subject and so remain[s] essentially unchanged by the reading experience."[29] A majority reader's attempt to "dominate" a minority writer's text can be interpreted as his or her refusal to read the text as a "stranger." The migrant writer who draws attention to the way in which the German language works, on the other hand, becomes the authority. By contrast, when the reading process is productive, "the self and other, reader and text, interact in such a way that the reader learns from the experience without losing critical distance; reader and text interact with a degree of mutuality. Foreignness is reduced, though not eliminated."[30] A reading that does not attempt to dominate a text written in Germany by an ethnic-minority writer will have to acknowledge the "multicultural identity" of the German language, as Biondi calls it in his essay. Similarly, the British reader, who is able to achieve a "balance of detachment and involvement"[31] in reading, will accept the grammatical and idiomatic differences in the various versions of English written around the world as an expression of such "multiculturalism."

Like Mamo, Akif Pirinçci's protagonist Akif in *Tränen sind immer das Ende*, is a member of the second generation,[32] and the construction of the "Turk" as someone who is uneducated and cannot speak German, is the focus of Pirinçci's criticism. But unlike Mamo, who is depicted as the ultimate victim of the system, and unlike Goethe's and Plenzdorf's protagonists, who both die, Akif survives his suicide attempt and decides to write his story. Although Akif does not get the girl, is not on speaking terms with his parents, and has no money, he has a good sense of humour, a vivid imagination, and "power over" the German language. Thus *Tränen sind immer das Ende* represents a humorous refusal to perpetuate the image of the migrant as "afflicted," as it[33] was constructed and theorized by Franco Biondi and Rafik Schami in their essay "Literatur der Betroffenheit"[34] and portrayed in the early guest-worker literature. Most of the texts of *Literatur der Betroffenheit* [Literature of Affliction] are first-person accounts of homesickness, suffering, alienation, and victimization, and the conditions under which migrants live and work in the Federal Republic are its main subjects. According to Biondi and Schami, the literature of guest workers – the two authors use the term "guest worker" ironically to expose its inherent contradictions – was to function as "self-help to defend identity."[35] They claim that affliction creates solidarity, since all migrant workers are subject to dislocation and discrimination, no matter what their country of origin. In these texts, migrant experience is constructed within the conventions of poetry, autobiography, and realist fiction, authenticity being the final objective.

With Pirinçci's refusal to adopt the literary discourse prevalent at the time of its publication, *Tränen sind immer das Ende* follows its model *Die neuen Leiden des jungen W.* (1973), a text that broke with the tradition of so-called literature of arrival ["Ankunftsliteratur"], which was the most popular form of literature in the GDR in the 1960s and 1970s. In these texts, arrival was to be understood as a protagonist's passage from alienation into a state of class consciousness signifying his or her "arrival" in socialism. Edgar Wibeau, Plenzdorf's protagonist, on the other hand, leaves his home and his workplace to become an artist. Apart from the fact that Pirinçci, like Plenzdorf, breaks with prevalent literary conventions, he rewrites the plot and character details of *Die neuen Leiden des jungen W.*, criticizes, like Plenzdorf, the education system, and uses language in an "oppositional" way.

Although Pirinçci alludes to Goethe's *Die Leiden des jungen Werthers* (1774) in his novel, he does not directly acknowledge his indebtedness to Plenzdorf. However, the parallels with regard to character and plot development between *Die neuen Leiden des jungen W.* and *Tränen sind immer das Ende* are hard to overlook. The protagonists Edgar and Akif are of the same age, they both fall unhappily in love with a young woman slightly older than they are, they run away from a small town to the city – Berlin and Cologne respectively – and temporarily attempt to reintegrate themselves into society, Edgar by joining the house painters' brigade and Akif by becoming a stagehand at the Cologne Opera. They both find substitute father figures, Edgar in the Bohemian Spanish Civil War veteran Zaremba, and Akif in Hassan, the spokesperson for the Turkish workers at the opera house. Furthermore, both Edgar and Akif aspire to find self-fulfillment as artists. Edgar draws, and at one point seeks admission to the Berlin College of Art. Akif writes film scripts and detective stories. Both are members of ethnic minorities: Edgar is of Huguenot and Akif of Turkish descent. Edgar's problems begin when, in an act of defiance, he drops a steel plate on the toes of his supervisor, who gives his French name a German pronunciation, and Akif gets into fights with people who distort his name to Akip, Akit, and Akük. And last but not least, both are members of the second generation.[36]

While Plenzdorf, through Edgar, criticizes the role of education and work training in the GDR as a tool of conformism, education in *Tränen sind immer das Ende* is satirized as a commodity and the basis of careerism. One of the first questions Christa asks Akif is whether or not he has a high-school diploma. He explains that he dropped out because he could not adjust to the German school system and blames the emphasis on rote learning and his "fascist German middle-class peers" for his fading interest in school. His exclusion from Christa's world – she comes from a middle-class family and is a law student – echoes the clash between aristocracy and bourgeoisie in *Die Leiden des jungen Werthers*. Although Graf von C. and Fräulein von B. both feel an affinity of mind and soul to Werther, they are not prepared to compromise the social order for his sake. Edgar's attraction to the idea of having aristocratic ancestors, on the other hand, is ironic not only within the context of a state that abolished class difference, but also within the context of the venerated reception of Goethe's text in the GDR.

Akif is painfully aware of the class difference between himself and Christa: "Was this the end? Mindless, hard and crippling work? At the same time, I knew that it couldn't go on with Christa the way it had. She, a future judge or lawyer and me, a stupid blockhead of a stagehand."[37] The text suggests that as a young Turk in Germany, Akif is predestined to spend the rest of his life in a menial job. On signing his contract with the Cologne Opera, Akif concludes: "I became what my father had predicted all along and had always tried to protect me with all his might from becoming: a worker."[38] Hassan discourages Akif from taking the job:

"Son, that's no work for you. Not for a young man. The opera kills you. You won't be able to take it. Look at me, my son! I've been working here for seventeen years. That's what a man looks like who has been working here for seventeen years."[39] Ironically, labour in the service of German culture has a debilitating effect on the Turkish worker's body and mind. Hassan suggests that Akif return to Turkey, marry his daughter and take care of his goats. His assumption that Akif is "enough of a Turk" to be able to lead this kind of life subverts the German stereotype of the "Turk." Pirinçci makes it sufficiently clear to the reader that the return to Turkey is no alternative for Akif. It takes, after all, a stretch of the imagination to picture the streetwise and popculture-smart Akif among the goats in the Turkish countryside. Throughout the book, Akif refers to himself as a Turk. With this strategy of representing himself as other, he undermines the power of the stereotype. The self-ironic identification with an ethnic group that elicits automatic prejudice in Germany parallels Edgar's repeated critical self-references such as "like an idiot, " "moron that I am" with which Plenzdorf satirizes the socialist practice of public self-criticism.

Contemporary GDR critics who approved of Plenzdorf's text, comment on his innovative use of language to express the emotions and thoughts of the young GDR workers ["Arbeiterjugend"]. Negative criticism from the GDR, on the other hand, almost always entailed a critique of the irreverent treatment of the classical model ["das klassische Vorbild"]. Critics thus found fault with Edgar's equating of his "sufferings" with the urge to empty his bowels when urinating. Furthermore, in *Die neuen Leiden des jungen W.*, the clash between the generations manifests itself in the juxtaposition of the atrophied language of the older generation with the humorous and subversive language of the young. Oppositional practice is at work in Edgar's rearrangement of well-worn phrases and proverbs and in his creative use of quotations from Goethe. When Plenzdorf critics talk about the second generation and the revolutionary impact of its language, they automatically think of Edgar and his friend Willi and not of the well-adjusted Dieter and Addi. What Plenzdorf seems to envision is a young generation of critically thinking new socialists with a disregard for ossified rules and a certain degree of individualism.

Akif's language is much more explicit about bodily functions than Edgar's – in the absence of censorship the West German reading public of the 1980s was used to much coarser language in literature and film than that of the East – and is intended to provoke the West German reader on a different level. Xenophobia, especially towards Turks, increased in West Germany when it became obvious that a fairly high percentage of the guest workers wished to stay and have their families join them. At that time, analogies between hostility towards Turks and anti-Semitism in Nazi Germany were already frequently drawn in discourses about the construction of Turkish identity in Germany. While Edgar's language is provocative by apparently treating Goethe irreverently, Akif's language is provocative through its evocation of Germany's Nazi past.

The book opens with a description of the discotheque where Akif meets Christa: "The name of the joint was ... Treff and it was packed like Dachau."[40] Akif also describes his fellow students' attempt to take it out on one of their teachers as follows: "They teased him calling him names until they were blue in the face."[41] Christa casts an "Auschwitz-like glance" at Akif whenever they are at odds. Thinking about his deteriorating relationship with her, Akif can suddenly see the "final solution" ["Endlösung"], a word, which apart from conjuring up images of the Holocaust, also alludes to both the title of Pirinçci's book and the playful use of "ende" ["over"] at the end of the Werther quotations on the tapes that Willi receives as secret messages from his friend Edgar. By repeatedly, apparently innocently, referring to concentration camp atrocities, Pirinçci, through Akif, not only demonstrates how language can be abused but, more importantly, also hints at the possibility of history's repeating itself in Germany.

While Franco Biondi employs strategies of defamiliarizing the German language by breaking grammatical rules and placing words in unfamiliar contexts, the colloquial German that Pirinçci uses in *Tränen sind immer das Ende* undermines the German reader's alleged educational and ethnic superiority by being overly familiar. The German reader may feel compelled to ask how a writer from the "outside" can so effectively write from the "inside." Furthermore, Pirinçci/Akif not only has a thorough knowledge of the German "masters," as is evident from allusions and quotations, but also of world literature. Akif lives through books, and he affirms his identity by drawing on the characters in the books he reads. Just as Akif attempts to affirm his identity by reading not Turkish, but mostly German and American literature, Pirinçci, a migrant writer intending to assert himself within German literature, needs to deterritorialize (Deleuze/Guattari)[42] both the literature of the "masters" and "the language of Goethe." By constructing his narrative both self-reflexively and intertextually, Pirinçci subverts the authentic and realistic discursive practices of migrant literature promulgated by Franco Biondi and Rafik Schami. With *Tränen sind immer das Ende* Akif Pirinçci makes the case that in order "to come of age," migrant literature needs to embrace issues other than homesickness and discrimination and adopt a narrative mode that distinguishes itself from social realism.

2 (Post)colonial Picaresque: Kerstin Jentzsch and Thomas Brussig

First-person point of view, confessional mode, episodic structure, a naive antihero, frequently of unknown background, whose many masters attempt to teach him about life, and a satiric aim are usually identified as some of the major elements of the picaresque narrative. Accordingly, Akif Pirinçci's *Tränen sind immer das Ende* could also be read as a present-day version of this narrative type. Like many other picaresque antiheroes, his first-person narrator finds himself either at loggerheads with members of the dominant group or exploited by them. And like many of his contemporary brothers, Akif is a likeable character who gains the reader's sympathy because he does not lose his sense of humour in the midst of life's adversities. Kerstin Jentzsch and Thomas Brussig, writers of the younger generation in what used to be the GDR,[1] who, unlike their older colleagues, are not held responsible by "West" Germans for not having attempted to topple a repressive political system, depict their protagonists as struggling with feelings of dislocation and inferiority similar to those suffered by Mamo and Akif. By adopting picaresque strategies both Jentzsch and Brussig satirize the colonization process of the GDR by the FRG as well as the corruption of the GDR's political system and the acquiescence of their parents' generation.

In the western world, the picaresque narrative has emerged in places faced with a national crisis and in need of a redefinition of national identity. From a Spain that was losing its status as a world power and whose aristocracy was threatened by the rising middle class, the picaresque made its way to Germany on the eve of the Thirty Years' War. In the wake of World War II, the genre flourished once more with novels such as Thomas Mann's *Bekenntnisse des Hochstaplers Felix Krull* [*Confessions of the Swindler Felix Krull*] (1954), Günter Grass's *Die Blechtrommel* [*The Tin Drum*] (1954), and Heinrich Böll's *Ansichten eines Clowns* [*The Views of a Clown*] (1963). Not only do these novels express the fundamental alienation typical of the picaresque, but they also attempt to come to terms with historical dislocation and the loss of cultural tradition.

In the 1970s and 1980s, the picaresque lost its attraction for FRG mainstream writers while it became popular among those writing from the "margins." As in many other multicultural societies, the picaresque has been adopted by German migrant writers to criticize mainstream society for condoning social injustice, xenophobia, racism, and imbalance of power among the various groups of society.[2] In his controversial novel *Rubinsteins Versteigerung* [*Rubinstein's Auction*], published in 1989, German Jewish writer Rafael Seligmann, for example, presents an antihero with a temperament and outlook on life comparable to that of Akif. His protagonist Jonny, aka Jonathan-Isaak, regards himself as a victim of the "negative German-Jewish symbiosis"[3] and questions, in a fashion reminiscent of Alexander Portnoy's "complaints," the relevance of Jewish tradition for young Jews in contemporary Germany.

In the GDR, on the other hand, the picaresque novel with its satirical tone and inherent criticism of society was not compatible with social realism in the service of socialist education, for this demanded an authentic and historically concrete representation of society in its revolutionary stages.[4] When GDR writers resorted to the picaresque mode to criticize society, the targets of their criticism used to be bourgeois western values rather than the socialist system. As William Walker has shown, the first volume of Erwin Strittmatter's *Der Wundertäter* [*The Miracle Worker*] (1957), for example, uses satire to "reveal the incongruities and contradictions inherent in bourgeois ideology,"[5] without, however, endorsing socialism. The novel concludes with the pícaro's flight into exile on a small Greek island. Manfred Bieler's *Bonifaz oder der Matrose in der Flasche* [*Bonifaz or the Sailor in the Bottle*]

(1963), on the other hand, moves beyond a critique of the bourgeois exploitation of the worker by satirizing "the relativity and changeability of people's allegiances and 'virtues' in light of self-interest."[6] With his defection to the Federal Republic in the wake of the Soviet invasion of Czechoslovakia, Bieler seems to have acted, in accordance with the principles of his criticism of *any* political system repressing individual rights and freedoms.

GDR fiction reached a new phase with Irmtraud Morgner's novel *Leben und Abenteuer der Trobadora Beatriz nach Zeugnissen ihrer Spielfrau Laura* [*Life and Adventures of the Troubador Beatriz as Chronicled by Her Minstrel Laura*] (GDR 1974/FRG 1976). By incorporating fantasy and mythology in her prose, Morgner subverts the claims of the dominant culture and criticizes the myths of patriarchal history from a feminist point of view. Morgner was also the first GDR writer to raise critical questions about gender relations and to protest against the censorship of any art that portrayed sexuality and eroticism.[7] The picaresque in its function as antigenre provided an appropriate mode for Morgner's rewriting of androcentric genres like the medieval quest romance and the classical *Bildungsroman* and its GDR variant, the novel of arrival.[8]

The picaresque also comes to the fore in postcolonial societies, particularly in the wake of periods dominated by realist or social realist fiction, as Ronald Blaber and Marvin Gilman demonstrate in *Roguery: the Picaresque Tradition in Australian, Canadian, and Indian Fiction*. Most "Western" critics have looked at the GDR as a society colonized by the former Soviet Union, which imposed not only its political but also its cultural values on its satellite states. While West Germany has officially been a postcolonial nation since it was granted full sovereignty by the occupying powers, many argue that the GDR's colonization by the former Soviet Union and its doctrines has been replaced by "West" German (neo)colonization of the "East."[9] Wolfgang Dümcke and Fritz Vilmar, for example, conclude: "If one does not equate colonization with the invasion of troops ... but keeps in mind the essential, namely the destruction of a 'native' economy, the exploitation of the available economic resources, the social liquidation not only of a country's political elite but also of its intelligentsia, and the annihilation of the developed – problematic as it may be – identity of a people, the GDR has indeed been colonized."[10] GDR citizens are expected to integrate into "West" German society, adopt "Western" standards, and regard their own cultural values as obsolete, in other words, shed their "old" identities. West German stereotyping of East Germans as backward, naïve, and provincial, coupled with the accusation that GDR citizens blindly and willingly supported a police state, has created an identity crisis for a people as well as for its literature.

West German critics generally conclude that GDR literature is anachronistic and premodern. Bernd Hüppauf, among others, advises East German writers to liberate their language and lose their fear of modernity."[11] The heated discussions over the status of "East German" literature escalated in the well-documented literature debate ["Literaturstreit"] in the summer of 1990, in which West German literary critics, most prominently Frank Schirrmacher, Ulrich Greiner, and Karl-Heinz Bohrer, argued against socially committed literature giving it the derogatory label of *Gesinnungsästhetik* [politically motivated aesthetics]. Concomitantly, established GDR authors have come to question their national and literary allegiances. While Günter de Bruyn, for example, chooses Brandenburg as a "liberating *Heimat*,"[12] Lutz Rathenow wonders:

What am I? A GDR citizen or a German? Am I East European because of my political socialization or Middle European in terms of mentality? Through my book I declared myself a Berliner. East Berliner or Berliner? Or is my Thuringian background more influential than I have been prepared to admit ... As a German-speaking writer, I feel that I have more in common with Swiss and Austrian writers than with writers from the FRG. But I also feel closer to Polish and Czech literature, with its often irreverent and critical attitude, than to GDR literature. What am I?[13]

Literature written by established GDR writers after unification has been concerned with a reassessment of the past as well as with problems of integration. As Roger Woods points out, "it is striking just how many projects are based on reconstructing biography,"[14] the attempt to explain what life in the GDR was like. Furthermore, according to Nancy A. Lauckner, the ways in which established authors treat problems of integration "largely continue established practices of the individual authors,"[15] that is, these writers choose the same strategies to represent integration problems with which they depicted GDR problems. Stefan Heym's *Auf Sand gebaut* [*Built on Sand*] (1990), Helga Königsdorf's *Gleich neben Afrika* [*Right Next to Africa*] (1992), and Rolf Schneider's *Volk ohne Trauer* [*A People Who Do Not Mourn*] (1992), to name only a few, all focus on the economic ramifications of unification and West German exploitation of the East. Apart from dealing with the economic injustice caused by unification, the "older" generation's texts published after unification are concerned with the Stasi debate and its aftermath, that is, with identifying those responsible for and complicit in upholding a deformed state socialism. "Status melancholicus" is the term Wolfgang Emmerich uses to describe the common aspect of post-unification literature with its focus on the disillusionment resulting from the failure of the socialist promise.[16]

The younger generation that Jentzsch and Brussig represent has, however, very different perspective on unification and consequently adopts different strategies to write about it. While Kerstin Jentzsch's novel *Seit die Götter ratlos sind* [*Since the Gods Haven't a Clue*], published in 1994,[17] has not received much public attention, Thomas Brussig's *Helden wie wir* [*Heroes Like Us*], published a year later, has been reprinted many times and will soon be released in its filmed version. The lack of acclaim for the first book and the exuberant reception of the latter are not indicative of differences in the literary quality of the two texts. In fact, both novels show the compositional and stylistic weaknesses of first books and are burdened by the weight of their intertextuality. Intertextual dialogue with "West" German and American works of fiction has become a trademark of post-unification writing from the eastern part of Germany. This dialogism can be interpreted as an oppositional strategy in itself, in that it writes back to the monologism imposed on GDR literature by government censorship.

Furthermore, while the extraordinary commercial success of *Helden wie wir* may be explained to some extent by the text's semierotic nature, Jentzsch's protagonist Lisa Meerbusch proves herself a true pícara to no lesser degree with regard to her sexual appetite and promiscuity. However, one reason that Brussig's novel has been selling better than Jentzsch's can be ascribed to his narrator's satirical comments about Christa Wolf and about her narrative *Was bleibt* [*What Remains*] (1990). Wolf's narrative, which records a day in the life of a woman writer under surveillance by the Stasi, added new fuel to the literature debate: What "will remain" of GDR literature and what kind of moral legitimacy can it claim? After it became public that between 1959 and 1962 Wolf had been involved with the Stasi, she was accused of portraying herself in this text as a victim of the system.[18] Many critics, particularly Germanists in the USA, contend that Wolf's role in the debate was that of a scapegoat. However, for the majority of the German literary establishment, as well as the German public, Christa Wolf lost her status as a dissident writer who chose not to emigrate in order to speak the truth of an oppressed people, and is now widely looked upon as a representative of a discredited political system. Once this system disappeared, Christa Wolf seems to lose her nimbus and become obsolete. While Brussig rewrites Wolf's text in the second half of his book in a satirical manner from the perspective of one of the young Stasi agents spying on Wolf's narrator, Jentzsch's allusions to Wolf's *Kassandra*, *Kassandra: Voraussetzungen einer Erzählung* and also *Der geteilte Himmel* [*The Divided Heaven*] (1963) are more subtle and less confrontational.

The chapter headings in *Seit die Götter ratlos sind* count the days before and after unification, a strategy which not only parodies the convention in early picaresque novels of assigning dates to episodes, but also satirizes the documentary impulse that used to propel much of GDR literature. The book opens fifty-nine days after unification with Lisa Meerbusch's departure to Crete on her twenty-fourth birthday, where she spends about six months in an attempt to relive the adventures of Zorba the Greek and to find herself. Through flashbacks, the reader learns that the most important person in Lisa's life was her uncle Willi, who worked for the Stasi and used to shower Lisa with extravagant gifts from the West. At the end of the novel, after Willi's murder, it is revealed that he and not his brother, as Lisa was brought up to believe, is her father. The relationship between Willi and his brother, who is a family judge and no less corrupt than Willi, is tense while that between him and Lisa borders on the incestuous.[19]

While family life is portrayed as unhappy in *Seit die Götter ratlos sind*, Lisa's relationships with young men from both the East and the West are equally unsatisfactory. The former leave her to begin a new life in the West, a plot detail reminiscent of the relationship between Rita and Manfred in Wolf's *Der geteilte Himmel*, and the latter, for whom she is an exotic creature, use her for sexual adventure. A few months before unification, Lisa quits her job as a teacher, because she was forced to make self-betraying compromises. She then works as a secretary and "native informant" for a couple of entrepreneurs from the West who attempt to convince GDR citizens of the validity of what they call "the concept for the improvement of the economic infrastructure of the GDR," according to which GDR citizens would buy the apartments in which they were living to be able to make a profit after unification. It is ironic that as a school teacher Lisa finds it morally objectionable to submit to the doctrines of a state that attempts to prevent all manifestations of nonconformism,[20] while she has no qualms about serving the "capitalist" system and enjoying the perks that come with the job. The money Lisa earns working for the West German organization as well as the fall of the Wall make it possible for her to travel to Greece. A few months later, her uncle Willi's violent death brings millions of laundered dollars into her possession, and she decides to return to Germany.

Like *Seit die Götter ratlos sind*, Thomas Brussig's *Helden wie wir* uses the family as a place and a trope to analyse and satirize both the GDR citizens' relationship with the authorities and the German-German relationship. Family life in its everyday regimentation, its predictability, and its adherence to petty rules is portrayed as reflecting the state's infantilization of its citizens with its promise to care for them provided they subordinate themselves. While Klaus Uhltzsch's relationship with his father, who like uncle Willi works for the euphemistically labelled "Ministry of Foreign Trade," is characterized by mutual contempt, that with his mother, who works as a hygiene inspector, can best be described as Oedipal. She smothers him with her love and cripples his masculinity with her overly protective and controlling behaviour.

Helden wie wir, like many picaresque narratives, employs the confessional mode to relate Klaus Uhltzsch's pseudoautobiography. The book's seven chapters are written as transcriptions tape-recorded for Mr. Kitzelstein, a reporter with *The New York Times*, who upon examining video material of the events of the night of the fall of the Wall, discovers Klaus Uhltzsch's crucial involvement in these events. As it happens, the Wall was not torn down by heroic people; rather, Klaus Uhltzsch's giant penis was instrumental in their liberation.[21] The narrative setup of *Helden wie wir* recalls that of Philip Roth's novel *Portnoy's Complaint* (1969), in which Alexander analyses with Dr. Spielvogel his "disorder," that is, his obsession with masturbation, which quenches all ethical and altruistic impulses in him. Portnoy is convinced that his Jewish background is as much responsible for his problems as is his mother. The analogy that Brussig draws between his protagonist's situation and that of Portnoy, a second-generation Jewish American who longs to sever his links to Judaism and to assimilate into the mainstream, is provocative. While immigration usually widens the gap between generations, it tends to widen even more between Jewish survivor parents and their American-born children, as it is fraught with trauma. Brussig's analogy suggests that the burdened relationship between Jewish American survivors and their children can be compared to that between parents of the GDR founding generation and their children. Although this relationship may be emotionally complex, it certainly is so for different reasons.

Brussig's protagonist blames his parents' generation and Christa Wolf, who for him is representative of all the writers of her generation, for their strategic silence, acquiescence, and lack of resistance. This criticism culminates in the last chapter of the book called "Der geheilte Pimmel" ["The Recovered Dick"], a title that rhymes with that of Wolf's *Der geteilte Himmel*, with Brussig's quotation of a speech that Christa Wolf delivered on 8 November 1989, one day before the fall of the Wall. In this speech Wolf encouraged GDR citizens not to give up on socialism with the words: "What can we promise you? No easy, but a useful and interesting life. No rapidly gained material wealth, but involvement in great changes."[22] Klaus Uhltzsch mistakes the speaker for Jutta Müller, the coach of the famous GDR ice skater and gold medal winner Katarina Witt, his mother's idol and "mother of all mothers." This title, according to Klaus Uhltzsch, seems to come naturally to her as her first name rhymes with "Mutter" [mother]. Incensed by the speaker's, and by proxy all GDR mothers', equation of socialism and duty, he intends to rush the podium to demand freedom for all. Tripping over a placard on a broomstick, he severely injures his genitals and has to undergo surgery which results in the abnormal growth of his penis, a phenomenon that Klaus Uhltzsch associates with the "great changes" predicted in Wolf's speech. Meanwhile, realizing his mistake in having confused Jutta Müller with Christa Wolf, he comes to the conclusion that the essential statement "the Wall has to go" was never uttered by Wolf. Consequently the German literature debate was pointless since no one can do political justice to an author who has never committed herself to a clear political opinion and hence cannot be accused of having written "Gesinnungsästhetik."

Furthermore, the analogy between Alexander Portnoy and Klaus Uhltzsch presents Brussig's antihero, and all GDR citizens with him, as victims of crimes against humanity. With this analogy, Brussig ironically undermines one of the GDR's founding myths with which it meant to distinguish itself from the FRG, namely the clear break with the Nazi past which made antifascism the prime criterion for early GDR literature. As Peter C. Pfeiffer points out, "when minister president Hans Modrow declared on February 8, 1990, that the GDR had to share in the responsibilities of German history (which was a euphemism for the Nazi past), he inadvertently signalled the demise of a separate national identity of the GDR."[23] Stasi agent Klaus Uhltzsch, however, compares German acquiescence and blind obedience to Nazi rule with that of the GDR citizens' under the rule of the SED [Socialist Unity Party] and the Stasi. Brussig's antihero satirizes their call for a nonviolent revolution in which he sees violence defined not so much as avoidance of bloodshed and property damage, but as moralizing prohibition of justified aggressiveness. In this way, the insistence on nonviolent confrontation appears to be the expression of an authoritarian personality.[24] Consequently, Klaus Uhltzsch does not use the power of his erect penis to push over the wall aggressively, but to hypnotize the guards at the Bornholmer Straße crossing point. By opening his pants and exhibiting himself, he transforms one of the guards into a passive tool of the revolution who unlocks the gates that Klaus Uhltzsch pushes open for the people.

While Brussig's pícaro thus describes himself as the "missing link of recent German history,"[25] Lisa Meerbusch ironically sleeps through the eventful part of the night nursing a headache. When she ventures across the border early in the morning, two Turkish men, who with a smile call themselves her guardian angels, show her the way. Upon returning the following day to pick up her welcoming money, she realizes that the Turks are the only people "welcoming" her to the "West." With her description of a group of East Germans' looting of a Sarotti chocolate truck whose driver is dressed as the Sarotti Moor – a figure reminiscent of Germany's brief flirtation with colonialism in Africa – and of West German "neocolonial" behaviour towards migrants, Jentzsch satirizes West German orientalization of the East Germans. East Germans are shown as uncivilized, rigid, and unsophisticated as compared to the flexible and dynamic West Germans, qualities that characterize them as unfit to compete in a free market society. As Lisa realizes when she is working for the couple from the West, she is expected to initiate personal change like a character in a *Bildungsroman* in order to become more like them. In a rather patronizing manner, her boss's wife gives her all kinds of advice about how to look and behave less like an East German.

One of the reasons that Lisa decides to begin a new life in Crete is that, as she puts it, the Cretans do not care whether she is from the East or the West. And indeed, the Cretans, not yet used to travellers from countries behind the Iron Curtain, do not differentiate between "East German" and "West German." On the other hand, they treat her like any other female German tourist travelling alone, that is, they approach her as a woman seeking sexual relations with Greek men in accordance with the stereotypical view of the "West" German woman on vacation. Ironically, Lisa is stripped of her "East" German identity by a "West" German double. Georgia, who rents the upper floor of her house to Lisa, takes her for a resurrected young "West" German, who used to live there before she drowned in the ocean twenty-five years earlier. Rummaging through piles of West German magazines from the 1960s, which she finds in the attic of Georgia's house, Lisa discovers a photograph of the drowned woman, who bears an uncanny resemblance to her. Lisa comes to realize that she, three decades later, is reliving, at secondhand so to speak, the 1960s travel experiences of West German women in search of sexual freedom and self-expression.

Another reason why Jentzsch's pícara chose Crete as her destination is that "West Germany" ceased to be an erotic space soon after unification. As John Borneman puts it: "For several weeks … after the opening, the erotic differences were explored in a series of both spontaneous and organized private encounters, parties, and ceremonial gatherings. Within six months, however, the two sides stood naked before a disassembled border, and with this uncovering, the erotic investment in the other was gone."[26] And ironically, by seeking an allegedly not yet charted erotic space, that is, Crete, Lisa learns that "West" German women have already "conquered" this space for themselves. Waking up in the idyllic cottage of the attractive shepherd Michaelis who found her rendered unconscious by the midday heat, she believes that her erotic fantasies of being selected as "his woman" have finally come true. However, Lisa learns that she is not his erotic love object when he asks her to write letters to a number of "West" German women to inform them when he will be available for sexual pleasures in the coming season.

In having her protagonist travel to Greece, Jentzsch also rewrites Christa Wolf's *Voraussetzungen einer Erzählung*. She echoes Wolf's combination of lectures and text in her own novel by interrupting the narrative chapters with chapters in which the gods, assembled in a tavern in Crete, comment on the unification process as well as on Lisa's actions. Yet the character of the adventurous Lisa Meerbusch who uses her physical attraction to gain advantages that make her trip more comfortable and who lives by the rules of Zorba the Greek, contrasts sharply with the character in Wolf's travelogue. Wolf's character, delayed at the East Berlin airport, passes her time reading the *Oresteia* to prepare for the trip to Greece. Unlike Lisa, who has never been outside the GDR, Wolf's narrator is ill at ease and almost paranoid during the short flight as well as during her sightseeing tours through Athens, in spite of previous travel experience in the West. Her obsession with mythology and classical literature in general and Cassandra's fate in particular makes it impossible for her to absorb new impressions and to interact in an unbiased manner with her environment. And unlike Jentzsch's pícara, Wolf's narrator feels threatened by displays of what she calls "aggressive virility" which for her is representative of the "patriarchal south."[27] For Wolf's narrator, the present obviously does not live up to the past. She even dismisses two American travel companions' enthusiasm about evidence of a prehistorical matriarchal society in Crete as reactionary, since such evidence from the past only highlights women's inequality in the present – which is nothing to rejoice about.

With the creation of Lisa Meerbusch, an enthusiastic, unprejudiced traveller who lives in the present and enjoys life, Jentzsch criticizes as life-denying the GDR predilection for the classical past, as celebrated in both the texts of its most respected writers and in school curricula. In Brussig's more satirical text, his antihero at the age of ten, attempting to get some straight answers from his mother about the facts of life and penis length in particular, is referred to the encyclopaedia entry on Greece with its pictures of heroic statues. The penises of the gods and heroes, as his mother explains, were depicted as small in order not to offend against the classical ideal of beauty, a comment that leaves her son stunned by this educational leap from anatomy to art history.

Both Jentzsch and Brussig also write back to certain linguistic phenomena peculiar to GDR German which served the main purposes of propaganda and indoctrination. As Derek Lewis observes, "by 1989 the political stagnation of the SED was reflected linguistically in two ways. Firstly, at the time when the Party needed to be most informed about the mood of its members, internal communication became totally ritualized; this had the effect of stifling essential dialogue ... Secondly, the SED-controlled media reacted to reformist pressure in a language which was wholly inappropriate: they either reiterated tired formulae about the *gute Entwicklung des Sozialismus* and *Einheit von Kontinuität und Erneuerung*,[28] or reverted to the strident rhetoric of the Cold War."[29] The most obvious of the various "streamlining" strategies in GDR discourse is that of juxtaposing several nouns to create a chain of associations, most evident in political slogans.[30] For example, in *Was bleibt*, Christa Wolf's narrator, inspecting the cultural centre at which she is giving a reading, looks at a sign that says "Growth, Wealth, Stability"[31] and ponders its significance. The juxtaposition of these three concepts implies both their logical connectedness and their interchangeability. In the taxi to the Athens airport on her return to Germany, Lisa, trying to imagine how she could spend the money that she "inherited" from her uncle, opens his final letter to her. The Stasi man's words are ironic if one considers Lisa's excitement about the money: "You are at your Greek beach thinking about the origins of civilization, of democracy, and of the human soul. At times, you are aware of your personal condition, your powerlessness, and your helplessness."[32] Furthermore, Lisa's concrete ideas, of how to spend the money, such as distributing it among senior citizens, buying new technologies, and building apartments, write back to the utopian dimension of Wolf's narrative texts and that of the speeches she gave before the fall of the Wall. Many members of the younger generation looked upon such ideals as empty promises.

The central preoccupation of the narrator in Wolf's *Was bleibt* is the development of "a new language," a language that will liberate itself from its colonial fetters by shedding its ideological baggage. However, the narrator makes it clear that the time for her to speak this other language has not yet come, an observation uncannily echoing Dr. Aziz's conclusion in E.M. Forster's *A Passage to India* that the time is not yet ripe for friendship between an Indian and an Englishman. Wolf even discourages a young woman writer[33] from publishing a manuscript since "every single sentence in it is true" and it therefore could "take her back to jail."[34] Writers in their thirties like Jentzsch and Brussing grew up with a literary discourse that, like Wolf's narrator's, did not dare to liberate itself. Caught between the colonial past and the postcolonial, and at the same time neocolonial, present, these writers struggle to find their own language.

Ronald Blaber and Marvin Gilman demonstrate how writing in the postcolonial context becomes progressively more pluralistic by moving away from monovocal utterances that are usually associated with colonialism. And as Helen Tiffin puts it, the "re/placing of carnivalesque European genres like the picaresque in postcolonial contexts, where they are carried to a higher subversive power,"[35] is one of many strategies of writing back to the European "masters." Both *Seit die Götter ratlos sind* and *Helden wie wir* return to a literary genre that, because of its critical and subversive potential, the alienation of its protagonist from society, and, in some cases, its erotic content, was not in favour in the society in which Jentzsch and Brussig grew up. The picaresque is also one of the most ambiguous genres and as such an appropriate vessel for the ambivalent feelings about unification and life in a free market society that Jentzsch and Brussig voice through their protagonists.

3 Re-Placing Language: The Poetry of Zehra Çirak and José F.A. Oliver

Both Zehra Çirak and José Oliver employ a variety of the textual strategies, such as allusion, code-switching, interlanguage, neologism, and syntactic fusion, identified by the authors of *The Empire Writes Back* as characteristic of postcolonial discourse. Çirak and Oliver position themselves within German discourse in a way comparable to that in which anglophone postcolonial writers position themselves within the discourse of the colonizer, but subversion of language operates differently in German than it does in English. In "Enge oder ein Versuch, Amerikanern Deutschland zu erklären" ["Narrowness or an Attempt to Explain Germany to Americans"], Chaim Noll claims that in contrast to the constrictions and restrictions that the "outsider" experiences as characteristic of German culture, the German language facilitates "expansion and digression."[1] Thus, according to Noll, German, unlike many other languages including English, has a systemic potential for resistance. It is this centrifugal force within the structure of the German language that Zehra Çirak and José Oliver exploit in their poems to abrogate the "centrality" of standard German and to inscribe difference.

When Chaim Noll refers to the oppositional potential of the German language, he is obviously thinking of its inflectional nature, that is, the fact that German expresses grammatical relationships through morphology rather than position in the sentence as analytic languages like English and the Romance languages do. The Polish-born Australian poet Ania Walwicz, for example, resorts to placing parts of the sentence in unidiomatic positions, using incorrect punctuation as well as repetition, to satirize official discourses about Australia. In "no speak," Walwicz deconstructs the stereotype of the inability of non-Anglo-Celtic immigrants to communicate intelligently by representing immigrant discourse as simplistic and childlike: "i no speak english sorry i where is john street where it is where please ticket and sixpence name what is dog what is house mary has a dog and a house."[2] In "New World," she undermines the dominant culture's pressure on newcomers to turn "Australian" by having the immigrant persona in her poem speak in self-imposed denial of his or her past: "I'm newborn. I'm new. Brand new. New. Me. I'm new. It doesn't matter what happened before. Now I'm new. I'm going to start a new life. Go to a new state. Make a clean. Break. With my past."[3] And, as Sneja Gunew has demonstrated, in her poem "europe," which parodies the discourse of travel writing and Australian notions of Europe, Walwicz "catalogues European diversity metonymically ... as consisting of rich food"[4]: "i'm europe deluxe nougat bar i'm better than most i'm really special rich and tasty black forest cake this picture makes me think of germany make me made me europe made me i keep my europe i europe this town is just like my polish town where born where is where am here is europe all the time for me in me i europe i keep it i got i get it in me inside me is europe."[5] Apart from the fact that Walwicz's language games are culture specific, that is, they comment on Australia and the relationship between the dominant culture and non-Anglo-Celtic minorities in that country, the structure of the English language dictates the form which rewriting can take.

Zehra Çirak and José Oliver, on the other hand, create semantic, and consequently cultural, ambiguity in their poems through the playful and subversive combination of morphemes. In "Duden Ichden"[6] for example, Çirak satirizes the controversial German spelling reform as reflected in the Duden reference texts, a reform which assumed nationalist overtones with German unification.[7] In the final lines of the poem, Çirak alludes to these nationalist feelings as well as to the stereotypical German preoccupation with order and conformity: "Now like then one dreams of the task of locking up spelling for the entire territory."[8] By substituting "zu riegeln" "to lock up" for "zu regeln" "to regulate," Çirak alludes to notions of confinement, finality, and rigidity. The subversive insertion of the letter "i" into the word "regeln" and the polysemy of "Aufgabe," which could be read either as "purpose" or as "abandonment," also show that written language, often removed from immediate context and the speaker's intention, is more prone to miscommunication than spoken language. The substitution of "lock up" for "regulate" also suggests that the two activities might have something in common: stagnation and inflexibility. In addition, the first stanza makes playful use of polysemy, easily created in German through the combination of prefix and word stem or of two nouns, in order to contrast the creative and subversive potential of the language with the attempts to eliminate ambiguity through rules. The title "Duden Ichden," which, depending on intonation, can be read either as the name of the *Duden* reference book plus a non-sensical rhyming word, or as meaning "you take this one, and I take that one," playfully overturns "central" notions of language based on *Duden* German.

José Oliver undermines the rules in a similar manner. In his poem "eingefallen/aufgefallen,"[9] the lyric speaker quotes Marco B. as declaring that the only way to be subversive in Germany is to not function.[10] Following Marco B.'s advice, the lyric speaker claims that he turned into a nomad within languages and guards life between the words.[11] With the neologism *Lebenswache* [guard of life], Oliver pits his own language variant against the High German standard. He uses neologisms in almost all of his poems as one of the major strategies to emphasize alterity by defamiliarizing the familiar.

The stanza discussed above also subtly adheres to the rhythm of Spanish, Oliver's "other" language. The authors of *The Empire Writes Back* refer to the adaptation of vernacular syntax to standard orthography as "syntactic fusion" and consider neologism a specific form of it. They point out that "successful neologisms in the english [*sic*] text emphasize the fact that words do not embody cultural essence, for where the creation of new lexical forms in english [*sic*] may be generated by the linguistic structures of the mother tongue, their success lies in their function within the text rather than their linguistic provenance."[12] The "German" idea of what it means to function, and along with it the grammar of standard German, are thus relativized and the value of neologisms such as *Lebenswache*, which could be dismissed as nonstandard German, lies in their success as metaphors. German then proves to be not the embodiment of some kind of cultural essence but dependent on a specific cultural context.

An even more explicit way of foregrounding cultural distinctions than syntactic fusion is code-switching, that is, moving back and forth between two or more languages. When switching codes, the author may either offer a translation of the words or passages written in the language with which the intended audience might be unfamiliar, that is, gloss the text, or refuse to translate the words in the "other" language. As the authors of *The Empire Writes Back* point out, "the choice of leaving words untranslated in postcolonial texts is a political act, because ... glossing gives the translated word, and thus the 'receptor' culture, the higher status."[13] In the first stanza of "Allianz,"[14] Çirak playfully juxtaposes the German and the Turkish words for "hand": "Hand" and "el." Combined, these two words form the German word "Handel," which means primarily "trade." The first part of the poem makes fun of the Germans' penchant for spending their vacations in southern Europe, vacations many can afford because of the strength of the German Mark. The greed of German tourists is satirized through the repetition of "viel," "much," in a grammatically incorrect position, a syntactic characteristic ascribed to Turkish speakers of German: "Summer exchange and relaxation at the ocean there we get sun much and warmth much and even more for our good money."[15] The extended metaphor of sexual intercourse to describe the relationship between Germany and its southern European partners, namely as copulation between their currencies, introduced in the third stanza, is reiterated in the second half of the poem. The relationship between the partners is reduced to a business transaction in which, however, they all lose to allegorized trade. "Allianz," apart from literally meaning "alliance," also alludes to Germany's insurance giant. The poem concludes with the words: "Trade rubs its hands with glee – eline saĝlik."[16] The Turkish words, a blessing that literally means "health to your hand," remain untranslated.

While code-switching and the use of untranslated Turkish words are not among Çirak's major strategies, Oliver uses both Spanish and the Swabian dialect to undermine standard German in a number of his poems. In "Poet in zwei Sprachen" ["Poet in Two Languages], an essayistic preface to his collection of poems entitled *Heimatt und andere Fossile Träume* [*Heimatt and Other Fossil Dreams*], Oliver concludes that he is not a bilingual but a quadrilingual poet, the languages he uses being Andalusian, Alemannic, Spanish, and German. By making the point that the two regional dialects, Andalusian and Swabian, are independent language systems with idiosyncratic modes of conceptualizing and representing reality, Oliver contests the "centrality" of High German and Castilian Spanish. Furthermore, many native speakers of German who are not familiar with the Swabian dialect have difficulty understanding the passages in his poems that are written in this dialect, and might not be able to decipher the meaning of every single word. Oliver thus places native speakers of German in a position in which they will feel like strangers in "their own" language.

In "dorfidylle heimattduft" ["Village Idyll Scents of Home"], for example, in which the misspelled word "Heimat" contains the word "matt" ["exhausted" or "jaded"], the exchange between the lyric speaker and the saleswoman behind the sausage counter is recorded in Swabian dialect. The first stanza of the poem, written in High German, describes the lyric speaker's encounter with "the elegantly packaged bank clerk,"[17] "the counter pale postal clerk,"[18] and "the traditional parking ticket distributor,"[19] all three of whom are described as "officious calm correct composed as usual."[20] While many Germans may associate "Heimat" with the idyll of village life, the bank and post-office clerks as well as the police officer are icons of the "German" spirit of law and order: "Discipline and order make the day come alive."[21] The idyll of "Heimat" is thus described as resting on law and order. But the notion of "Heimat" is also founded on the dichotomy of the familiar and the unfamiliar, Germany and "Ausland," insiders and outsiders.

The saleswoman's comment that one should know better than to fall ill when on vacation outside Germany because one will always get short changed,[22] blurs the boundary between village parochialism and xenophobia and racism. The saleswoman's platitudes are interspersed with quotations from Goethe's *Faust*, quotations that have become platitudes, because they are so often used and misused in everyday speech. This strategy also ridicules the traditional habit among the older generation of Germans to sprinkle their conversation with quotations from the masters of German literature, particularly Goethe and Schiller, to support their personal opinions by the appeal to such authorities. The last two lines of the poem, "to be German, so a friend says, means to feel Goethe inside,"[23] ironically comment on the "German" policy of cultural exclusion, which is based on the notion that "real" appreciation of Goethe is part of the German genetic makeup and that Goethe belongs to the Germans.

José Oliver's collection of poems entitled *Gastling*, which was published in 1993, is his most political. It also contains more untranslated Spanish passages than his previous volumes of poetry. The word "Gastling," "guest," is a neologism formed in analogy to "Fremdling," "stranger," and ironically refers to the situation of second-generation migrants, who, although they were born in Germany, are often still treated like unwelcome guests. "Gastling" aptly reproduces the tension of this paradoxical situation. The first stanza of "Poem eines mir anvertrauten Gastlings" ["Poem by a Gastling entrusted to me"] is written in Spanish. It concludes with the speaker's apologies for having forgotten that he is in Germany.[24] The repeated statement "despierto," "I wake up," in the first stanza refers to the act of waking up as an awakening with no return: "An awakening as one can only wake up in Germany. As one has to wake up in Germany. As one is forced to wake up in Germany. As one is forced to wake up in Germany if one was born in this country but has never belonged."[25] The final stanza of the poem turns to the inevitable consequences of such cultural politics by alluding to the surge of firebombings and arson attacks directed against "foreigners" in Germany: "The taste of fire on the tongues. The smell is a fire that was set. Always is set. Self-guarded. Just words. Fire. The drunken laughter of the arsonists. The drunken laughter of the just."[26] These images of fire evoke the Holocaust and echo the poetry of one of the writers Oliver admires most: Paul Celan, whose Romanian Jewish parents were murdered in concentration camps.

Paul Celan's influence is even more apparent in Oliver's poem "im gerippe eines tages" ["in the skeleton of a day"] in the same collection. The poem connects Auschwitz with Hoyerswerda, Hünxe, and Mölln: "A death like Auschwitz still, not yet, what comes. The people's Germany, you, why? Do you permit? Let it be done to you? The place of death, the escape, the mark. Again on this forehead ... The German alphabet that could read differently. Reads the German People, belongs to our People, begins with H with H like M, in Hoyerswerda Hünxe Mölln."[27] In the triptych of poems "dreifacher tod zu Mölln I," "dreifacher tod zu Mölln II," and "dreifacher tod zu Mölln III" ["triple death in Mölln I," "triple death in Mölln II," "triple death in Mölln III] and in "buchstabe S" ["letter S"], poems about the attacks on German Turks in Mölln and Solingen, Oliver defies "German" attempts to pass over these deaths in silence.

While the majority of the poems in *Gastling* mourn the violent deaths of "foreigners" in Germany and associatively link the murders with the genocides of Auschwitz, Hiroshima, and Guernica, a number of poems in the collection *Weil ich dieses Land liebe* [*Because I Love This Land*] deal with the fall of the Wall and German unification. "Als die MAUER fiel" ["When the WALL fell"] and "klare absicht" ["clear intention"], for example, use the conventions of concrete poetry, in addition to punning, to reveal the disillusioning discrepancy between the intentions and the results of unification: "When the Wall fell, I was surprised. When the Wall fell, I had to compose myself. When the Wall fell, it left me stunned with joy. When the Wall fell and the national anthem was sung, I knew that when the Wall fell, the Wall stands."[28] This poem expresses the fear that many non-German permanent residents in Germany, as well as some people in neighbouring countries, felt in the face of the nationalistic fervour which triggered the surge of xenophobia and racism in the wake of the fall of the Wall.

Although allusions to specific political events are rare in Zehra Çirak's poetry, resistance to religious, governmental, or paternal authority is pervasive. In "Hut Ab" ["Hats Off"][29] Çirak satirizes the Catholic church's penchant for pomp and performance in the face of famine in countries in whose languages the pope, ironically, never fails to address the world: "God be with you, so they say, but what will happen if I don't meet him? Keep your regards, I think, and I know that no one will miss my 'hello.' I greet you, says the Pope almost flawlessly via satellite on each Easter in languages of most of the world. One hears him even in those of the least. Greet again, Pope, inwards, those who turn their hats inside out on days they have no reason to celebrate."[30] The poem "Militär" ["Military"] in the same collection criticizes recruitment policies and represents the common soldier as the victim of distorted patriotism: "One of them has to, and the other soldier voluntarily gives up his own free will. These are the Jumping Jacks of the nation. The string is the state, the same old way for the mother country, and the hands that play and fidget with the string, sometimes briefly pull it to drill and sometimes pull it for a longer time. These are the bigheaded heads, blockheads that make blocklegs run." [31]

Like the poems in which Çirak satirizes patriarchal institutions, the poems that deal with "European" complacency and insensitivity to the needs of the so-called Third World are intended to provoke the reader, and despite their playfulness, leave behind an uneasiness. In the short poem entitled "Flugzeugabsturz" ["Plane Crash"],[32] a major European pharmaceutical company responds to the appeal by a humanitarian organization to "drive out hunger, not humans" by sending off a jumbo jet loaded with diet pills. The poem "Euroegozentrismus,"[33] whose title ironically conflates Eurocentrism and egocentrism, equates "Europeanness" with uncharitable behaviour and preoccupation with personal wellbeing. The lyric speaker asks resignedly why she should be blamed for having already become one of the "well-fed and jaded" who, however, will not always be able to hide when the needy knock at their door: "Why should it be my fault that I'm already a European, one of the well-fed and jaded , one of the westernized, one that does not yet have to beg in order to survive, one of those who are condescendingly considering how the world, the rest of it, can be saved. One of those who won't be able to hide when they come to demand something like give me your daily bread and give me your bed, give up something of yourself for me."[34]

Although the speaker seems to find it difficult to resist becoming "Europeanized," and thus "Euroegocentric," she further explores her cultural identity in "Doppelte Nationalitätsmoral" ["Double National Morality"] and in "Kulturidentität."[35] "Doppelte Nationalitätsmoral" metaphorically refers to Germany as a cold shoe in which the warm Turkish foot does not feel comfortable when touching "hot ground," that is, hostile and potentially dangerous territory. The poem "Sich warm laufen" ["Warm-Up Run"] uses the metaphor of the bridge to describe the migrant's situation: "Because one knows that even bridges lead somewhere, one does not need to hurry when crossing them. Yet the temperature is always lowest on bridges."[36] In a move to undermine the perceived differences between "Turkishness" and "Germanness," Çirak defines cultural identity as cultural hybridity in her poem "Kulturidentität." The text begins with the speaker's attempt to define cultural identity by asking: "Is it something in which I will be able to recognize myself, or is it something with which others categorize me?" In the subsequent lines of the poem she clearly states her preference for cultural hybridity, which, on account of its ambiguity, undermines ethnic categorization: "I'd prefer to wake up Japanese on a futon in rooms with transparent make-believe doors. Then I would like to have an English breakfast, then work Chinese, with unfamiliar indifference, eagerly and diligently. I'd prefer to eat like the French and, gorged, bathe like the Romans. I would like to go on a Bavarian hike and dance African. I would love to have Russian patience and not to have to earn my money American. I wish I could fall asleep Indian like a bird on the back of an elephant and dream Turkish about the Bosporus."[37] Migrant life is depicted here as a chosen condition that transcends nationality, while the nation is seen as a space whose borders are subject to ongoing negotiation.

In contrast, José Oliver problematizes life between cultures in the final section of the collection *Auf-Bruch* [*De-parture* or *Break-Up*]. In the poem "Woher" ["Where from"], the speaker wonders: "Identity crisis is usually associated with the '2nd Generation.' Identity crisis. How can one speak of a crisis when there has never been an identity for us."[38] Where Çirak finds creative potential in the absence of a/one specific identity, Oliver's poem expresses both existential *angst* and a desire to bring about political change. His criticism of the German citizenship law is particularly fierce in his poem "Nationale Identität": "Yes, my Spanish passport has the following number: EC00835133. Conceived in Germany, imported from Spain. Ever since, I have been wearing an invisible tattoo, on display in some archive. After all, numbers bring nations together. And I have permission to exist. Since we have become this odd mixture of reference numbers and valid stamps, we have been allowed to live here. Thank you. How would I have otherwise found out who I am: EC00835133."[39] Like other poems discussed above, this poem evokes the analogy between the dehumanized bureaucracy to which Holocaust victims were subjected and that to which "foreigners" must answer.

Furthermore, the speaker's paradoxical statement: " I have been wearing an invisible tattoo, on display in some archive" conveys the migrant's dilemma of being both visible, in the sense of being seen as different, and invisible, in the sense of being excluded from a community of citizens that defines itself by ethnicity and thus practices a policy of exclusion. The latter is often closely linked with denial of access to public spaces and institutions. In "Public and Private: Immigrants and the Search for a Common Political Language," John Brady claims that the debate over the use of the Tiergarten, Berlin's main urban park, demonstrates how the migrant's visibility is linked to exclusionary policies. In the summer of 1997, the city of Berlin attempted to ban barbecuing and picnicking in the park because of complaints that weekend picnickers left behind an unsightly amount of litter. Since it is mostly "foreigners" who use the park, the Tiergarten controversy, according to Brady, shows that the attempt to deny "non-German" residents access to public areas meant depriving them of the opportunity to express cultural differences publically. Space, or alleged lack of it, also looms large in the discourse of the Republikaner, a radical right-wing party with obvious racist overtones, as Werner Schiffauer explains in "Europäische Àngste: Metaphern und Phantasmen im Diskurs der Neuen Rechten in Europa" ["European Fears: Metaphors and Phantasms in the Discourse of the New Right in Europe"]. While the National Party in the UK is preoccupied with the loss of Britain's sovereignty, and Le Pen's Front National in France with the loss of political independence, the German Republikaner believe that "foreigners" overburden and undermine the welfare state. Their phantom fear is the fraudulent and parasitic asylum seeker. According to Schiffauer, the fear that "foreigners" abuse the system is coupled with the belief that they feel no responsibility for the German state and therefore ruthlessly exploit it. He claims that this fear manifests itself in claustrophobia, the feeling that "the boat is full" or one is "sitting on a bomb." Consequently, migrants are often referred to as "sozialer Sprengstoff" [social dynamite].[40]

Both Zehra Çirak and José Oliver write back to such discourse by addressing these "German" phobias and by using images of narrowness and confinement as well as of bursting and explosion in their texts. In the sequence of poems "Spielplatz-Angst" ["Playground Phobia"], "Spiel-Platzangst" ["Play(ground) Agoraphobia"], "Spiel-Platz-Angst" ["Play-Ground-Phobia"],[41] for example, Çirak addresses the fear of cramped space by alluding to the stereotype of the "immigrant woman" as particularly fertile, a fertility which is to blame for overcrowded playgrounds. Further-more, through the puns in the titles of the three poems, Çirak draws attention to the fact that the word "Platzangst" in German, that is, agoraphobia, is commonly misused as meaning claustro-phobia. This folk etymology has its roots in the polysemy of "Platz" which means both "site/open space/square" and "burst." Usually, when German speakers refer to their "Platzangst," they refer to the physical anxiety created by a space that is experienced as too narrow. This physical discomfort is associated with the bursting of the body as a reaction to confinement.

In turn, Zehra Çirak and José Oliver respond to the cultural restrictions and confinements imposed on them and other migrant writers by the mainstream and the culture industry through the creation of their own space in the German language. According to the authors of *The Empire Writes Back*, "the crucial function of language as a medium of power demands that post-colonial writ-ing define itself by seizing the language of the centre and re-placing it in a discourse fully adapted to the colonized place."[42] Çirak and Oliver effectively contribute to dismantling traditional notions of what constitutes "German literature" through the pro-cesses of abrogation, that is, denying standard German its privi-lege, and appropriation, that is, taking the German language and making it "'bear the burden' of [their] own cultural experience."[43] Both poets use the "systemic potential for resistance," to which Chaim Noll draws attention in "Enge oder ein Versuch, Ameri-kanern Deutschland zu erklären," as a means of creating a place for themselves within German culture and literature.

4 Rewriting Home: The Border Writing of Barbara Honigmann and Renan Demirkan

As Hartwig Isernhagen has pointed out, borders are both "disjunctive" and "conjunctive": one can look at a border as a line of separation or as a space of "communicative relations."[1] American critics working in the field of Latin American, and particularly in Chicana and Chicano literature, see the "conjunctive" enacted in what they have named "border writing." In Emily Hicks's words, border writing expresses "an attitude on the part of the writer toward more than one culture ... emphasiz[ing] the differences in reference codes between two or more cultures."[2] Chicana writer and border theorist Gloria Anzaldúa, for example, gives voice to the new mestiza who celebrates the fragmented physical, national, and cultural experience of the mestiza consciousness and who lives in the spaces between the different worlds that she inhabits.[3] In Anzaldúa's utopian view of border culture, national identity becomes ambiguous and will ultimately lose its segregating power in favour of a culture of *mestizaje* and hybridization.[4] In like manner, border writing becomes a site of subversion through intertextuality and the mixing of languages and genres.

While the sociohistorical realities of both Jews and Turks in Germany are quite different from the Mexican American cultural experience of annexation, the notion of border writing nevertheless offers an interesting narrative model for a discussion of texts produced by members of these two minorities. Barbara Honigmann's

Roman von einem Kinde (1986) and Renan Demirkan's *Schwarzer Tee mit drei Stück Zucker* (1991) are situated at the borders of "Heimat"[5] and "Fremde", East and West, past and present, self and other, Christianity and Judaism, and Christianity and Islam respectively.

The story "Roman von einem Kinde," after which the collection of six interrelated short narratives is named, is set in East Berlin. It is written as a fictive letter[6] from the protagonist to her former lover and father of the child to whom she is about to give birth. The final story takes place in Strasbourg where the protagonist, like Honigmann herself, lives with her family as a member of the Jewish community. From her adopted country, France, the narrator retrospectively sums up in one sentence the significance of a migration motivated by the search for "Heimat": "I have landed here after a triple *salto mortale* without a net: from the East to the West, from Germany to France, and out of assimilation into the midst of Torah Judaism."[7] The six stories move along these three major axes: East and West, the two Germanies, Russia, Slovakia, France, and secular and orthodox Judaism. Each of them deals with the search for "Heimat" and, coincidentally, for personal and communal identity. The most literal search for "Heimat" is described in the story entitled "Wanderung," a word which translates into English as both "hike" and "migration." It also echoes the anti-Semitic myth of the Wandering Jew exiled from home and condemned to suffering. In this story, the narrator and some friends spend their summer vacation hiking through Eastern Europe. Although they have a detailed map, they lose their way, and, being unable to speak any of the national languages or local dialects of the area, are sometimes uncertain in which country they are. Their search for Galicia, the alleged cradle of East European Judaism, is likewise marked by failure, since, as the narrator points out, they do not know where to look for it.

During the hike, the narrator's non-Jewish friends argue over the degree of their parents' guilt regarding the Holocaust: "Always arguing about the same: about Hitler about Stalin about the Germans about the Russians about the Jews about the War about the East about the West and about our parents, particularly about our parents."[8] The narrator falls ill over these disputes and resumes the hike apart from her friends. The question of whether or not "East Germans" are less responsible for the Holocaust and its aftermath lies at the bottom of their coming to terms with the atrocities and their relationship with "East-German" Jews. As the official discourse of the GDR maintained that it was not a successor state to Nazi Germany, schoolchildren were taught that Erich Honecker had spent time in a fascist prison for resisting the Nazis while West German leaders had not. Honigmann's story thus addresses the ramifications of coming to terms with the Holocaust from both GDR and FRG perspectives as well as referring, if only implicitly, to the historical and ideological conflicts between German Jewry and East European Jewry. The title of the story "Wanderung" seems to allude to the essay "Juden auf Wander-schaft" ["Jews on Their Travels"] by Austrian Jewish writer Joseph Roth, himself born in Galicia, in which he describes not only the economic plight of Eastern European Jews and their being dis-criminated against by German Jews, but also their opposition to assimilation. "Wanderung," like the other five stories, makes it clear that past and present are inevitably interlaced and that the Holocaust continues to shape the relationship between Germans of either German state and Jews, as well as that between German Jews and Jews elsewhere in the world. In "Von den Legenden der Kindheit, dem Weggehen und der Wiederkehr" ["About the Leg-ends of Childhood, Leaving and Returning"], Honigmann com-ments on the impossibility of talking with Germans about "things Jewish" in a matter-of-fact way. She explains that, by moving to France, she attempted to avoid having to deal with this situation: "It is this conflict, this hysteria, from which I have run away. Here in France, things do not concern me as much; being only an observer, a guest, and a stranger liberated me from the unbearable closeness to Germany."[9] Interestingly enough, Honigmann does not distinguish between the GDR and the FRG in this essay.

Although *Roman von einem Kinde* was published three years before the fall of the Wall, the Wall is never mentioned, and the narrator's migration from East to West is not hampered by the geographic reality and the bureaucracy of national borders. In the title story, the narrator describes the search for the only synagogue in East Berlin, in which – obviously for the first time – she joins the small community with her baby son for Seder. The blessing at the end of the commemoration of the Jewish exodus from Egypt, "Next year in Jerusalem!" anticipates the narrator's move to Strasbourg. Because of its close-knit Jewish community, this city is often referred to as the Jerusalem of the West. Apart from the

fact that Strasbourg, unlike the GDR, has a vibrant Jewish community, it is also located in the geographical, political, and linguistic
borderland between Germany and France. In addition, Alsace has
become home to a large number of immigrants, particularly from
the Maghreb and from Turkey, who contribute to creating a truly
hybrid culture. The narrator seems to be drawn to this kind of
cultural hybridity and is able to live only in the border zone, as
is obvious from her revelation in the final story, "Bonsoir, Madame
Benhamou": "Now I know what it means to be foreign. This
vague feeling, which has always been with me, became a reality
here."[10] Her description of the "cheap" part of town where she
and her family live together with other newcomers, Africans,
Maghrebians, and Turks, in a way evokes Gloria Anzaldúa's provocative description of dwellers in the borderlands: "The prohibited and forbidden are its [the borderland's] inhabitants. *Los
atravesados* live here: the squint-eyed, the perverse, the queer, the
troublesome, the mongrel, the mulatto, the half-breed, the half
dead; in short, those who cross over, pass over, or go through the
confines of the 'normal.'"[11]

The narrator's/author's affinity to the borderlands is also
reflected in the narrative strategies of *Roman von einem Kinde*. The
text crosses not only the boundaries of fiction and autobiography,
but also those of other genres. Epistolary passages, quotations
from novels, poems, and songs, the text of a postcard and the
inscription on the tombstone of the family Scholem, as well as
allusions to numerous writers like Walter Benjamin, Gottfried
Benn, Johann Wolfgang von Goethe, Gottfried Keller, Heinrich von
Kleist, and Marcel Proust, contribute to the text's dialogic nature.
The book's title also echoes the titles of Bettina von Arnim's *Goet-
hes Briefwechsel mit einem Kinde*, Jurek Becker's *Bronsteins Kinder*,
and Christa Wolf's *Kindheitsmuster*.[12] As Anat Feinberg observes,
"all Second Generation writers ... write with a deep awareness of
the long German literary tradition. Works by Goethe, Schiller,
Gottfried Keller, or Wilhelm Busch are echoed in their texts,
indeed, they seem to be part and parcel of the spiritual biography of
these German-Jewish writers."[13] But it is Goethe's *Wilhelm Meister*
and Keller's *Der grüne Heinrich*, which both deal with their protagonists' quest for personal and communal identity, that serve as
major intertexts in *Roman von einem Kinde*. Yet Honigmann's allusion to these prototypical *Bildungsromane* highlights the differences

rather than the similarities between the two male protagonists' and the female Jewish protagonist's search for home. Germany will never be home to Honigmann's narrator, but she feels very close to German culture. Writing in German and paying homage to texts that have become an integral part of that culture helps the narrator to cross the border, both physically and spiritually.

In her comparison of the "mixed-language" writings of Gloria Anzaldúa and Irena Klepfisz,[14] Jane Hedley observes that borderland consciousness "produce[s] a conviction of being prophetically called to speech and to narrative" and claims that in both Klepfisz's and Anzaldúa's texts, "the protagonist regresses or descends or is driven to a zero-point of linguistic and cultural aphasia that is also a narrative zero-point, and then each recovers a sense of who she is through narrative."[15] Hedley argues that in many of the texts by women that are "obvious candidates for an emerging canon of 'borderland' writing," the protagonists "undergo an identity crisis from which they emerge into a new sense of who they are or what their life's purposes need to be."[16] In *Roman von einem Kinde*, the protagonist's "crisis" is the birth of her son Johannes. The birthing experience not only engenders the narrative process, but it also motivates her to join the Jewish community, to study the Torah, and ultimately, to emigrate to Strasbourg.

In the title story "Roman von einem Kinde" Honigmann represents the symbiosis of mother and unborn child as one of the rare moments of perfect union, locating "Heimat" within the narrator herself. During the weeks after her son's birth, the boundaries between her body and that of her child merged, so the narrator explains, and she was unable to tell if she was giving birth or being born [hence the ambiguity of the title]. The narrator describes this liminal condition, in which she "regresses" into a preverbal stage [Kristeva's "semiotic"][17] only to (re)enter the symbolic stage together with her son by relearning language in the process of teaching him word by word and thereby making sense of her life: "It is so beautiful that at first one lives speechless with one another and only slowly, together, discovers one word after the other, learning how to spell one's whole life."[18] The narrator arrives at the "zero-point of cultural aphasia" through the invocation of a dream about Auschwitz: "Once I had a dream. In it, I was in Auschwitz with all the others. And in the dream I was thinking: Finally, I have found my place in life."[19] This dream, along with an anecdote about her hiding from a non-Jewish girlfriend a news-paper photograph depicting a German soldier shooting at a Jewish woman holding her child, reveals the narrator's identification with the victims of the Holocaust. It also proves the impossibility of a true dialogue with the German Jewish friend. Consequently, in the final story, "Bonsoir, Madame Benhamou," the narrator fol-lows Gershom Scholem's advice not to stay in Germany. In "Dop-peltes Grab" ["Twin Grave"] Scholem suggests that the narrator and her husband emigrate to a country in which they can study the Torah: "Jerusalem would be good, New York would be good, London would be good, any place would be good, but Germany is no longer good for Jews. One cannot learn anything here, and therefore it does not make sense to stay."[20] And from her chosen exile, Honigmann joins Anzaldúa, Klepfisz, Renan Demirkan and other border writers in forging a new identity through writing.

As in *Roman von einem Kinde*, the narrative process in Renan Demirkan's semi-autobiographical novel[21] *Schwarzer Tee mit drei Stück Zucker* is instigated by a "crisis," in this instance, the pro-tagonist's waiting for a Caesarian section in a Cologne hospital. And as in *Roman von einem Kinde*, birth and rebirth serve as the central metaphors for the narrator's experience. Waiting to give birth triggers in the protagonist a process of remembering her own childhood and reflecting upon the childhood of her parents and grandparents. Her own "Reise ins Leben" ["Journey into Life"] [22] began with her father's departure to Germany, where he went to live as a guest worker and where his wife and two daughters joined him a year later.

The efforts of the two generations of Turkish migrants to feel at home in Germany are successful to varying degrees. The nar-rator's mother does not think of Germany as her home. All the same, during a brief return to Ankara she realizes that after twenty years she has become estranged from Turkey, to which she still refers as "Heimat." In "Die Brücke im Januskopf: Vom Altwerden in einem ungastlichen Land" [Bridging Janus: Grow-ing Old in an Inhospitable Land"], Renan Demirkan draws atten-tion to the dilemma of the first generation of migrant workers and their spouses in Germany. Having left their home countries because of economic instability or lack of political freedom rather than from personal preference, this generation is nevertheless bound to the host country through their children, who go to school in Germany and often do not speak their parents' first language. Although, according to Demirkan, the majority of first-generation Turks grow old in Germany, they prefer to spend the final years of their lives in Turkey.

Unlike his wife, the narrator's father finds his "Heimat" in German music and literature because of his "western" education. Demirkan's intention in creating a variety of responses to Germany in her characters, shaped as they are by their different personal histories, is to deconstruct the stereotypical image of the "Turk" as uneducated, fundamentalist, and unwilling to integrate. She also reminds the reader that the migrant's personal development prior to arriving in Germany plays an important role in shaping his or her relationship with the adopted country. The mother's experience of having grown up in a large traditional family in a rural environment is quite different from that of the father, who, having lost his parents at an early age, was raised in a boarding school and graduated from university with a degree in engineering. His university education and secular upbringing make it easier for him to feel at home in Germany and to make compromises in his daughters' education.

Although they do not receive much help from their teachers, the assimilation of the two girls is described as a spontaneous process. As the narrator points out, the borderline between "we" and the "others" becomes so blurred for the two girls in only two years that they adopt the customs of the people in the German village as their own. The wish of the narrator and her sister to be no different from everyone else provokes the dismay of their mother, a practising Muslim, particularly around Easter and Christmas, when the girls ask for Easter eggs and a Christmas tree. At school, however, the girls are alienated by their teachers' persistent questions about their "home country." Having gained more self-confidence during years of exposure to such insensitivity and gestures of exclusion, the eighteen-year old narrator learns to assert herself when asked about her country of origin. Her response undermines notions of fixed national identity: "I am a cosmopolitan." [23] As her parents' adjustment to their adopted country is different from her own, so is that of her sister. While her younger sister is introverted and obedient, the narrator is outspoken and rebellious.

If "returning home" to Turkey is often a disappointing and alienating experience for the first generation, the second generation, curious about its ethnic roots, can often only return as tourists.

The narrator's secret visit to Turkey with her German boyfriend is just as frustrating and alienating as Honigmann's narrator's search for Galicia. It even poses dangers to her personal safety. The narrator does not dare to contact her Turkish relatives since, in her mother's opinion, having moved out of the house against her parents' wishes, she lives in sin. Travelling with a boyfriend only aggravates the offence against their rules and expectations. But it is not only to her parents that she has become "non-Turkish." A young Turk, who offers the couple a place to spend the night, attempts to rape her and justifies his crime by telling her that by travelling with a German man she has forfeited her rights to be respected as a Turkish/Muslim woman.

Although Demirkan's narrator has access to "authentic" ethnic experience, at least vicariously through her parents, second-generation narrators often seem to look at Turkey through "western" eyes. In *Schwarzer Tee mit drei Stück Zucker*, Turkey is represented as both an exotic place of colours and spices, as well as a patriarchal society in which women, in accordance with religious beliefs, are raised to be docile servants to their fathers and husbands. Turkey is also described as a place where survival, especially that of women and children, is often accidental. Its representation as an undeveloped country is particularly apparent in the narrator's comparison of the technical efficiency of the German medical system with the inadequacy of the Turkish. The narrator's mother, lying unattended for hours in an overcrowded hospital in Ankara after her water had broken, survived only because the hospital's oxygen tent happened to be in the maternity ward on that particular day. Four years later, however, she lost her third child because the oxygen tent could not be located.

While Turkey is described as a world of "improvised survival," Germany is depicted as "functioning by the stop watch."[24] As much as German efficiency is portrayed as having its merits, such as in the safeguarding of health and life, it also makes everyday interactions between people sterile and even inhumane. The German nurse, for example, is depicted as rude and unfeeling, unlike her Dutch colleague who treats the patient with respect and sympathy. Furthermore, Germany is described as hostile to children with its fences and prohibitive signs. Obeying the signs that forbid stepping on the meticulously cut lawns in the neighbourhood, the girls resign themselves to playing inside the apartment.

Unaccustomed to the noise produced by the children's play, the owners give the family notice. The text also points at the injustice and discrimination suffered by Turkish labourers like the narrator's mother, who receives only a fraction of the money her German colleagues are paid for doing the same work.

German officiousness is epitomized in its bureaucracy as the narrator describes her experience at the local registration office ["Einwohnermeldeamt"]. Although she arrived during regular office hours to get a moving form ["Umzugsformular"] stamped and is the only person waiting, the clerk at the counter for "foreigners" ["Ausländerschalter"] ignores her. Attempting to catch the woman's attention, the narrator is rudely told to be quiet and sit down. This scene is one of many in German migrant literature, in which, according to Leslie Adelson "literary depictions of foreigners' collisions with present-day bureaucracy are not merely about German 'coldness' or post-modern alienation; they can and should be read as confrontations with a legacy of German racism and colonialism."[25] The interaction between the two women also illustrates the segregating function of language. The clerk addresses the narrator in "Gastarbeiterdeutsch" which apes the allegedly broken German of foreigners in order to emphasize the speaker's own superiority as a native speaker. This pidgin German, which is a construction of the German native speaker rather than an authentic rendering of nonnative usage, resorts to unconjugated verb forms and the informal pronoun to address the other. With its forced simplicity and informality, it reduces the addressee, who is constructed by the speaker as a member of a visible minority, to both child and foreigner status and is thus not only demeaning but also racist. The narrator, however, has learned to "talk back." The narrator's "talking back" in "Ausländerdeutsch" inverts the power relationship and challenges the construction of who is and who is not German. Demirkan's depiction of her narrator as a woman who refuses to be a victim breaks with the convention in texts by German Turkish writers of portraying Turkish women as such. This tendency is particularly apparent in Saliha Scheinhardt's stories and novels[26] and in films like Helma Sanders-Brahms' *Shirins Hochzeit*, Jeanne Meerapfel's *Die Kümmeltürkin* and Hark Bohm's *Yasmin*.[27]

While Demirkan depicts the first generation of German Turks as still being rooted in Turkey to a certain degree and the second generation as being alienated from Turkish culture and not accepted as Germans, her narrator envisages a "hybridized" future for her yet unborn daughter. With her mixed heritage as child of a German Turkish mother and an Austrian father, she will make her home in the borderlands by resorting to the various cultures at her disposal:

Listen to me: We will take the hill from my grandparents' village and put it next to the Rhine... then we build a corn-yellow canopy with stars and make it your place. With colourful kelims from Turkey, soft down pillows from Austria and cuddly stuffed animals from Germany, we will build the most beautiful bed on earth ... On weekends we will invite the whole family ... The songs that we will be singing together won't be sad. Then we will take the boat across the Rhine to the museum to see the Andy Warhol exhibition. If you don't like that, we will do everything the other way around: We will carry the Rhine, the Cathedral, the *Altstadt*, the museum and the potato pancakes to my grandparents' village and read poems by Goethe and Heine on top of the hill on the weekends.[28]

The narrator's crossing of the national borders between Turkey and Germany, her negotiation between Islam and Christianity, and the attempt to bridge the generation gap are reflected in the inter-textuality of *Schwarzer Tee mit drei Stück Zucker*. The two most conspicuous intertexts are a Turkish folksong, pinned on a piece of paper on the wall of a friend's apartment, and Jacques' speech in Shakespeare's *As You Like It*, recited by one of the actors during a rehearsal. In the folksong , the lyric speaker, addressing the Black Sea, mourns the loss of home and the separation from loved ones in Turkey. The passage in which the narrator recalls her friend and his colourful apartment immediately follows the recollection of her clash with German bureaucracy at the registration office. The sterility of the white hospital walls contrasts with the aquamarine carpets, yellow kelims, bluish-green curtains, and potted palm trees in the attic apartment. Her friend tells the narrator that it was important for him to reproduce the light blue of the Black Sea close to the shore, and the intense blue of the deep ocean, the borderline between life and death, as he puts it. The apartment thus forms a "heterotopic" space, in the sense that Michel Foucault uses the term in "Of Other Spaces." Foucault defines "heterotopia," in contrast to utopia, as the mythic and symbolic place of "else-where," in which the laws of time and place that rule the everyday world, lose their function or take on new meanings. In this way, the apartment constitutes a countersite, resistant to "German" ways of designing the urban environment.

While the description of her friend's apartment serves to high-light the sterility of the "German" environment, the quotation of Jacques' speech serves to expose "German" ways of instrumen-talizing art in the service of pragmatism and efficiency. Producer and stage manager agree to stage a *Reader's-Digest* version of the play, as the narrator puts it, in which Jacques' speech, with the exception of the first line "all the world's a stage, and all the men and women merely players," is to be omitted. In an act of rebel-lion, one of the actors recites the unabridged version of the speech, accusing the producer of "destroying utopia." The irony is that the actors during their discussion of the play reveal their own ambition, envy, and greed. They are oblivious to the fact that these are the exact vices that the characters in the comedy overcome to live in their utopian world of love.

Renan Demirkan also creates a voice in the novel that speaks for the ultimate other. The narrator's reminiscences are suddenly interrupted by a woman moaning in labour on the bed next to hers. All the narrator can see of the woman is her full black hair. Her black hair, her "ancient moan,"[29] and her deep voice, scream-ing the words "Maika! Tschi!" signify to the narrator that she is a "gypsy." Rather than reaching the "zero-point of cultural apha-sia" herself, the narrator experiences it vicariously through a woman who belongs to a group of people in German society who rank at the bottom in the hierarchy of foreigners. Sinti and Roma also remain the ethnic group most underrepresented in post-Holocaust discourse in Germany. The woman's voice and the untranslated syllables with their semiotic force [Kristeva] break the silence and disrupt the social order of the hospital.

With the exception of this one incident in *Schwarzer Tee mit drei Stück Zucker*, neither Renan Demirkan nor Barbara Honigmann resort to "bilingual writing" [the use of code-switching, interlan-guage, syntactic fusion, untranslated words and vernacular tran-scription], unlike many Chicana writers, such as Irena Klepfisz and Zehra Çirak. Although other second-generation German Jewish writers[30] use Yiddish in their prose, Honigmann, a native speaker of German, does not. The self-imposed simplicity of Honigmann's style is the result of her attempt consciously to avoid "the political jargon of the former GDR and likewise the trendy neologisms of the West," as she declared in a conversation with Guy Stern.[31] Striving for lucidity and "purity of language," Honigmann breaks with the trope of the "polluted" and "polluting discourse" of the Jew.[32] It was not Yiddish, which, as Gilman maintains, was recognized in Germany "as a separate and distinct literary language," but "mauscheln" – speaking German with a Yiddish accent – that "came to characterize the Jew as parvenu."[33] Speakers who "mauscheln" are, as Gilman puts it, "between cultures, and individuals represented as moving across boundaries are always understood as polluting and polluted."[34] In "On My Great-Grandfather, My Grandfather, My Father, and Me," Honigmann expresses her anxiety at not being listened to by the German audience:

I wanted to present myself completely differently than my great-grandfather, my grandfather, and my father, and now I saw myself, just like them, speaking again to the Other, hoping to be heard, perhaps even to be understood, calling to him, 'Look at me! Listen to me, at least for five minutes.' When I really think about it, the shortness of my texts has to do with the fear that people would stop listening to me if I spoke longer, that I only have a short time frame. I understood that writing means being separated and is very similar to exile, and that it is in this sense perhaps true that being a writer and being a Jew are similar as well, in the way they are dependent upon the Other when they speak to him, more or less despairingly. It is true of both that approaching the Other too closely is dangerous for them and that agreeing with him too completely will bring about their downfall.[35]

Like Barbara Honigmann, Renan Demirkan seems to be anxious to be understood by the German reader. While the former breaks with the trope of the "polluted discourse" of the "Jew," Demirkan breaks with the trope of "Turkish speechlessness." As Arlene Teraoka observes in discussing the portrayal of the "Turk" in the texts of mainstream German playwrights: "The Turk smiles, laughs, nods, shows hesitation, confusion, and even deliberation. But he never speaks."[36] Both authors demonstrate with their texts that attempting to be "heard" by the dominant culture as well as to challenge that audience's stereotypical perception is a necessary step towards undermining the majority's silencing mechanisms. As Barbara Honigmann and Renan Demirkan rewrite notions of "Heimat," placing it in the borderlands, they cannot avoid certain contradictions and ambiguities from becoming apparent in their texts.

5 Rewriting Autobiography: Lea Fleischmann and Richard Chaim Schneider

Barbara Honigmann's semiautobiographical writing is informed by the fact that she grew up in the GDR and has since chosen to live in France rather than in the FRG (chapter 4). I will demonstrate in this chapter that not only the relationship of German Jewish writers to Germany but also their generation plays an important part in shaping their texts, particularly those with autobiographical elements. German Jewish autobiography focusing on contemporary life in Germany is a fairly recent literary phenomenon. If one compares Lea Fleischmann's *Dies ist nicht mein Land: Eine Jüdin verläßt die Bundesrepublik* (1980) and Richard Chaim Schneider's *Zwischen Welten: Ein jüdisches Leben im heutigen Deutschland* (1994) with recent Jewish American autobiographies, like Eva Hoffman's *Lost in Translation: A Life in a New Language* (1989),[1] certain major differences are immediately apparent. These differences can be attributed to the authors' having grown up in different societies and the particular histories of their adopted countries vis-à-vis the Holocaust but also, less obviously, to the role that autobiography has played in mainstream and minority writing in Germany and the United States.

All three authors are the children of East European Jews – both Fleischmann's and Hoffman's parents were born in Poland, Schneider's mother in Hungary and his father in Czechoslovakia. But while Fleischmann's and Schneider's parents decided to stay in post-Holocaust Germany, Hoffman's parents emigrated from Poland to Canada in 1959. As a consequence of the different relationships that Jewish Americans and German Jews have had with their respective countries, the two German Jewish autobiographies deal with disassimilation whereas Hoffman describes assimilation. *Lost in Translation* celebrates Americanization through education and the acquisition of idiomatic American English, looks back nostalgically and uncritically at Jewish life in post-Holocaust Poland and is relatively unconcerned with Jewishness. Both Fleischmann and Schneider, on the other hand, are preoccupied with what Dan Diner has called "the negative symbiosis between Germans and Jews after Auschwitz."[2] They efface their Polish or Hungarian and Czech origins, and view their Jewishness in racial but also in religious and cultural terms.[3] Although both authors mention in passing that their mothers did not speak German well, their growing up in a language that is not the language spoken at home – Hoffman's central topic – is not an issue in either autobiography.

Autobiographical writing has not only been one the of prevalent genres in American mainstream literature but also in Jewish American, African American, Latino/Latina and other ethnic minority writing. Hoffman's text thus not only is part of a rich tradition of East European Jewish autobiography in the United States but is also one of numerous contemporary autobiographical texts written from a variety of "ethnic" perspectives. Some of these texts combine different discourses, for example, autobiography and ethnography in Zora Neale Hurston's *Dust Tracks on a Road* (1942), Richard Rodriguez's *Hunger of Memory: The Education of Richard Rodriguez* (1982), and David Mura's *Turning Japanese: Memoirs of a Sansei* (1991), or autobiography and popular translation theory in Hoffman's own book. That all these texts rely heavily on essayistic writing, which recasts the autobiographical, can be attributed to the fact that, as Arnold Rampersad points out, the relationship between the private self and the community in autobiography is predicated on a moral vision. The community acknowledges the individual's sacrifice of privacy "in order to elevate the community as a whole" through the autobiographic act.[4] Although, within the context of German minority writing, the autobiographies of Nsekuye Bizimana *Müssen die Afrikaner den Weißen alles nachmachen? [Do Africans Have to Imitate Whites in Everything?]* (1985) and

Chima Oji's *Unter die Deutschen gefallen: Erfahrungen eines Afrikaners* [*Fallen under/among the Germans: An African's Experience*] (1992)
also adopt essayistic/journalistic discourse, Fleischmann's and
Schneider's autobiographies are, together with Chaim Noll's
Nachtgedanken über Deutschland [*Night Thoughts about Germany*]
(1992), the first German Jewish autobiographies to combine the
two modes of discourse.

Lea Fleischmann's provocative autobiography *Dies ist nicht
mein Land* is divided into three parts: "The door is being sealed:
Schma Israel," "I had a German passport, but I was not a German," and "I lived five years with them: Enough."[5] She rewrites
the conventional structure of Holocaust autobiography – life
before camp, initiation to and endurance of camp life, and escape
from the camp – with a twist. As someone born in 1947 who
spent her early years in a camp for displaced persons, Fleischmann is obviously not writing Holocaust autobiography. Yet,
by imaginatively linking her own life with the Jewish generation that perished, Fleischmann makes the Holocaust central to
her text.

Lea Fleischmann opens her book with the question: "Where
does memory begin?"[6] and locates the origins of her memories in
a small Polish village in 1937, ten years before she was born. What
follows is the description of Jewish community life with a happy
family at its centre: A father, a mother, and a girl child, with whom
the autobiographical self identifies, welcoming the Sabbath by
lighting candles. One day, German soldiers invade the village and
force the Jews on to a train. What follows is a nightmarish account
of deportation and a merciless selection in the camp that destines
the old and the very young to the gas chamber.

The second section of the book juxtaposes the fictive account of
the Holocaust atrocities described in the first part with Fleischmann's own childhood in camp Föhrenwald. In her early childhood, Fleischmann saw the world as inhabited by Jews and by
Nazis, and the stories with which she grew up could not have
been more brutal and shocking: "I learned about Jews who had
to dig their own graves before they were shot, I learned about
mothers whose children were torn from their arms and beaten to
death in front of their eyes, I learned about gassing before I knew
what gas was, I learned of dogs which were trained to kill
humans, I learned about children who were thrown alive into the

fire pits."[7] Apart from shaping Fleischmann's childhood memories, the Holocaust significantly affected her life in other ways. Since her grandparents and all her father's and her mother's siblings died in the Holocaust, Fleischmann describes her life as deprived of Jewish tradition and the culture of East European Jewry. Fleischmann's parents, like Schneider's, belong to the group of approximately twelve thousand displaced persons, Jews from East Europe, who decided to stay in Germany rather than emigrate to Israel, North America, or Australia. Furthermore, as a teenager she not only felt cut off from the past, but also from the future. As hardly any children survived the Holocaust, it was difficult for teenage girls to find suitable boyfriends. While in narrative terms her life in camp Föhrenwald corresponds to the section in Holocaust autobiography dealing with life before camp, section three corresponds to the phases of initiation and endurance anticipating Fleischmann's "escape" to Israel. Fleischmann concludes her book by drawing the provocative analogy between the five years that her mother spent in German concentration camps and the five years that she spent as a teacher in the German school system: "My mother lived five years among/under the Germans, and I lived five years with them. Enough."[8]

In the third, and most essayistic/journalistic section of the book, Fleischmann describes the German school system as a world of paragraphs and rules that instill fear in the students and break their will. In her critical analysis of schooling in Germany, she comes to the conclusion that since German students continue[9] to be educated to obey orders rather than to think critically and independently, a repetition of the Holocaust cannot be ruled out. She supports her argument with detailed examples of her colleagues' intolerance, pettiness, and fear of life. Fleischmann asks herself how highly educated and intelligent adults, who are afraid to confront their headmaster and other authorities, and who blindly follow regulations that might prove inappropriate, could be considered qualified to educate the young. As it is the time of the antiterrorist laws ["Berufsverbot" and "Radikalenerlaß"], teachers who dare to be critical or are politically active are directly or indirectly penalized for their nonconformism. The students, however, are the real victims. Fleischmann cites the example of one teacher who failed all students who missed a test because of a school-wide demonstration. She had announced the test a week before and therefore, according to the rules, was not authorized to cancel it. At least one student's promotion to the next grade was jeopardized by this unfair treatment and the teacher's narrow-minded, though bureaucratically correct, behaviour.

Fleischmann juxtaposes her analysis of educational practices, which is based on her observation of everyday situations in her life as a teacher, with stories she has been told by survivors and with her own mental images of Holocaust atrocities. She thus compares the subservience of civil servants in the FRG with Nazi Germany's blind submission under Hitler's rule, present-day materialism with German greed for Jewish money during the Third Reich, and the insistence on discipline inside and outside the classroom with the meticulous killing operations in the death camps. In sum, Fleischmann describes her time as a teacher not only as a process of learning more about "the Germans" – she points out that during her time as a university student, she was still living in "Jewish isolation"[10] – but also as a process of unlearning conformism.

The education she received from her parents seems to have equipped her with an inclination for "oppositional practice." Her own education, the principles and values of which she depicts as representative of Jewish education, contrasts starkly with that of her German schoolmates. While the educational practice of the German parents was characterized by a pull-yourself-together pedagogy, which left little room for feelings, her mother was convinced that she was a weak and sickly child and therefore had to be pampered. Disarmed by her tears, her parents were unable to punish her physically, a common practice among German parents, as Fleischmann points out. As a teacher, she used to recall her father's Old Testament tales of wisdom such as that of Abraham "talking back" to God and God giving in to him, and this gave her the power to contradict her headmaster. Her experience in the German school system taught her how important it is to resist unreasonable rules and regulations. Resistance is essential for Jewish survival anywhere and at any time because, as Fleischmann concludes, identifying with those who perished: "We had to dig our own graves, he [Jesus] died without resistance, and we let them massacre us without resistance."[11] In retrospect, however, her initial pedagogical idealism, which made her believe she would be able to bring about change, seems to have been misplaced. Fleischmann decided that she did not want to spend the rest of her life attempting to solve the problems of the Germans and to make them more human, so she emigrated to Israel.

Lea Fleischmann's and Richard Chaim Schneider's autobiographies, apart from using a different tone – Schneider's is less emotional and confrontational – differ in their approach to the "German/Jewish symbiosis" and in their responses to living among "the Germans": emigration to Israel and conditional commitment to Germany. But most significantly, Schneider's text is not directly concerned with the Holocaust. Generational differences – Schneider is ten years younger than Fleischmann – influence the genesis of these two autobiographies. Schneider identifies with the generation to which Reinhard Mohr refers to as "Zaungäste" ["spectators"], "the generation that came after the revolution," that is, the generation born between the baby-boomers and Generation X. Typical of the generation of 1978, according to Mohr, is that "unlike the generation of 1968 and the postmodern 'neonkids,' it has not developed a political or cultural symbolism that would make it immediately identifiable ... It is the mark of this generation that it stands with one leg in history and with the other in a presumably futureless present."[12] While resistance/opposition ["Widerstand"] is a key concept in Fleischmann's text, Schneider observes that he is one of the few Jews of his generation to speak out publicly: "Micha Brumlik, Henryk M. Broder, Lea Fleischmann, Michael Wolffsohn and whatever the names of the Jewish figureheads of the German media may be, they all are approaching age 50. We, however, who are about to turn 40, seem to be silent."[13] Schneider's autobiography can be read as an attempt to break this silence.

Zwischen Welten is comprised of a brief preface, prologue, six chapters and an epilogue: "Fassbinder," "Displaced Persons," "Hellas," "Germany," "Israel, and "Hear, Israel."[14] The book's subtitle, *Ein jüdisches Leben im heutigen Deutschland*, explicitly announces its subject matter, and the six chapters explore German Jewish identity from different angles. Although the indefinite article *Ein* in the title seems to be an indication that Schneider declines any representative role as a spokesperson for the German Jewish community, he does discuss a collective historical experience and uses the pronoun "wir," "we," whenever he refers to his generation. He also claims in the prologue that his Jewish socialization in Germany exemplifies that of other second-generation German Jews.

While the preface and the epilogue demonstrate the degree to which Jewish identity in the Diaspora, particularly the German Diaspora, is affected by current political events, the prologue highlights the problematic situation of German Jews who live in the country that committed genocide against the Jewish people. The six chapters place the German Jewish Diaspora within not only a historical/political, but also a spiritual, religious, and cultural context. In the preface, Schneider explains that the fall of the Wall and German unification changed his original plan to write a book about world-wide Jewish secularism. The revival of anti-Semitism and the rise of neo-Nazism in the wake of unification forced Schneider to reconsider his own position as a Jew in Germany, and he decided to focus on "the cultural and emotional background"[15] of second-generation German Jews. Schneider points out that to present the problematic situation of German Jewish existence from an insider's perspective, he selected autobiographical details only in so far as they serve to illustrate certain aspects of Jewish identity in Germany. In the epilogue, Schneider claims that the peace negotiations in the Middle East and the historic handshaking between Yassir Arafat and Jitzschak Rabin in Washington, 13 September 1993, initiated a process that would eventually make the Diaspora meaningless,[16] and Jews all over the world would have to decide to what extent they still felt committed to Judaism. Schneider thus frames his account of Jewish existence in the German Diaspora, as exemplified by his own biography, with two historic events: German unification and peace in the Middle East. This framing device mirrors Schneider's and his generation's position between worlds: between East and West, Germany and Israel, German culture and Jewish culture, secular and orthodox Judaism, and, last but not least, between generations.

However, as Schneider maintains, the turning point in the relationship between Jews and Germans is marked by an event that took place four years prior to the fall of the Wall: Jewish protest against the staging of Rainer Werner Fassbinder's play *Der Müll, die Stadt und der Tod* [*Garbage, the City and Death*] (1976) on the day of its première at the Schauspielhaus in Frankfurt on 31 October 1985.[17] A small group from the Frankfurt Jewish community occupied the stage just before the play was to begin, unfurling a banner which read "Subventionierter Antisemitismus"[18] ["subsidized anti-Semitism"]. Fassbinder's play, loosely based on Gerhard

Zwerenz's novel *Die Erde ist unbewohnbar wie der Mond* [*The Earth Is as Uninhabitable as the Moon*] (1972), deals with the controversial plan developed in the late 1960s by the city of Frankfurt, together with a business consortium led by large banks, to transform the Frankfurt Westend [German spelling] from a residential into a commercial neighbourhood. The protagonist of the play, the Rich Jew, who is an unscrupulous speculator in real estate and responsible for the destruction of the historic Westend, also gets away with strangling a prostitute. As Ruth K. Angress claims, "wherever possible Fassbinder improves on Zwerenz by making his Jew more drastically repulsive" and by implying that "if there is anti-Semitism the Jews bring it on themselves."[19] The general tenor of the discussion in the leading German newspapers about whether the play was anti-Semitic and whether performances should be banned, was to exonerate Fassbinder from the charge of intended anti-Semitism, but to concede that his play might rouse anti-Semitic feelings and should therefore not be performed.[20] Schneider explains that the "Fassbinder-Affäre" had two immediate effects, one communal and one personal: It proved that Jews are justified in maintaining the binary opposition Jew/German,[21] and it shook him into awareness.[22]

Schneider's re-vision of German Jewish identity prompts a re-vision of the exhausted form of conventional autobiography in his text. While conventional autobiographies usually open with the birth and childhood of the writer and frequently culminate halfway through the book in some kind of conversion experience, Schneider chooses to begin with the relation of his own "conversion" experience, triggered by the Fassbinder affair, a "conversion" from the belief that a Jew can be both a Jew and a German, to the realization that "being a Jew in Germany turned into a manifestation of Otherness."[23] Living in Vienna at the time of the controversy, Schneider at first felt not only geographically, but also politically removed from the event. Most important, he refused to identify with the protesters and felt only embarrassment and shame on their behalf:

Inside me something was appalled by the pictures that were shown: An elderly gentleman told the TV reporter in broken German how he had suffered in the concentration camp; young Jews, foolishly proud, were singing 'Am Jisrael Chai' – the Jewish people lives. I began to feel ill at ease; I did not want to have anything to do with this. I felt ashamed for being lumped together with these people. I am not like them; I've become emancipated, and I know how to act like a true democrat ... I can even speak proper German. I am not a Jew from the shtetl. I do not look like a Jew. I am tall, strong, do not have a crooked nose, and I know how to behave properly."[24]

The degree of anxiety in Schneider's emotional reaction to the fact that Jews in Germany had suddenly become visible is evident in his construction of the "Jew" in conformity with the stereotype of the East European Jew as inferior, uneducated, unemancipated, and physically identifiable. This image contrasts with Schneider's construction of his own identity, which he discusses in the three subsequent chapters. As mentioned above, Schneider's father was born in Czechoslovakia and his mother in Hungary. He also points out that one of his grandfathers died in the Holocaust. The chapter, "Displaced Persons," however, is not concerned with family history. It focuses instead on the clash between two cultures, German culture and a "pragmatic" version of Chassidism,[25] with which the young Schneider, growing up in Munich, had to come to terms. He humorously refers to the contrast between the private world of following Jewish Law and the public world of everyday interaction with the Germans as the "border between gefilte fish and veal sausage."[26] Schneider explains that one of his earliest lessons in Jewish identity was given him by Moische Gerczik, an Auschwitz survivor whom he regularly saw at the synagogue. Each time that the young Schneider attempted to rush by him, Gerczik would stop him and ask him his name. "Richard," the boy would answer proudly, an answer that never satisfied Gerzcik and would only make him repeat his question. "Chaim Jossel!," the only appropriate answer in the eyes of Gerzcik was then rewarded with a smile and a candy.

Richard Chaim Schneider draws attention, in this chapter, to the second generation's identity crisis, which resulted from growing up between cultures and which was exacerbated by the trauma of their being the children not only of survivor parents but, more significantly, of survivors who decided to live in the country where the atrocities had taken place. The majority of East European Jews chose to emigrate to Israel and the New World hoping that geographical distance would also ensure a mental distance from the events of the past. "Settling in Germany, on the other hand," as Cilly Kugelmann claims, "offered a paradoxical advantage: precisely the proximity to the country and to the society responsible ... permitted a fictional new beginning, a kind of Jewish 'Zero Hour' that avoided the (probably impossible) mental task of accepting the past ... Keeping the memories alive could be projected, as it were, onto the environment, which could never permit one to forget what happened."[27] She adds that living among Germans "provided a further paradoxical advantage: the need to have an unambiguous victim-perpetrator relationship."[28] Having grown up in this atmosphere seems to have made Schneider depend on, or at least long for, this "unambiguous victim-perpetrator relationship." The fact that in the first sentence of the book he expresses his concern about the blurring of the borderlines between friend and foe caused by the fall of the Wall, and that he draws attention to the confusion of the victim-perpetrator relationship in the wake of the Fassbinder controversy, makes this longing evident.

While Schneider focuses on his religious education during his childhood in "Displaced Persons," in "Hellas" he talks about the relevance of his high school and university training. As children of parents who grew up in East Europe, the second generation was immersed in a cultural heritage, as Schneider points out, that was not their own: "The challenge was to conquer the most important bastions of western culture at one and the same time: Athens and Rome and Berlin."[29] This chapter clearly reveals the paradoxes in Schneider's and his generation's education. On the one hand, his parents were proud when he became an expert on Goethe and Schiller and encouraged him to absorb German culture; on the other hand, they had second thoughts about his assimilation: "If our son succeeds in the German *Gymnasium*, then he too will belong to the master race, and then he is no subhuman. Here is yet another contradictory statement: stand your own ground; we Jews also have worth today. Become German, because only then do you actually belong to the master race, but under no circumstances assimilate."[30] Henry L. Feingold, who contributed to the anthology *The German-Jewish Legacy in America 1938 to 1988: From "Bildung" to the Bill of Rights*, would probably argue that Schneider and his parents are trapped by the German Jewish legacy of *Bildung* whose assets are usually identified as self-discipline, will, and energy.[31] Feingold's suggestion that this concept of *Bildung* "is a new form of basically secular identity formation which gives high priority to intense individuation, autonomy, and the internalization of controls," and that someone striving for *Bildung* is the "kind of person [who] does not easily perceive himself as a member of a flock of which God is the shepherd,"[32] can be read as a warning that "Jews" who strive to confirm their identity through *Bildung* will have to be careful not to betray part of their Jewish identity. How intricate the balance of allegiances can be is exemplified by Schneider's own life. After having adopted German citizenship, he was called up for military service and fortified himself with a novel by Günter Grass while waiting for the reply to his request for exemption from service in the military: "I was now clinging to it, to this other Germany in which I so much wanted to believe and to which I felt I belonged."[33] When Schneider was writing *Zwischen Welten*, he was apparently oblivious to the charges of plagiarism against Günter Grass who incorporated a passage from Edgar Hilsenrath's autobiographical Holocaust novel *Nacht* (1978) into his own novel *Das Treffen in Telgte* [*The Meeting in Telgte*] (1979). Sander Gilman calls Grass's "borrowing" a "violation of the Jew's authenticity, of the voice of the Jew narrating his own experience."[34] Gilman persuasively argues that because *Nacht* was published only with great difficulty in Germany – *Night*, the English translation of the text, appeared in 1967 – while *Das Treffen in Telgte* was widely promoted and discussed, "Grass manages to incorporate and thus make invisible, not only his source, but certainly as important, the context out of which this source springs, the postwar German Jew's struggle to establish his own identity in German culture."[35] Only later in life did Richard Chaim Schneider realize that it was true that he knew the books of the gentiles much better than the books of his own people, as a delegate of the Chabad movement in Munich pointed out to him.[36] An anecdote which relates his failure to read a text in Hebrew at a family gathering in Israel, a shortcoming which earned him his father's embarrassment and the reproachful stares of the Israeli part of the family, serves as evidence. Nevertheless, against the wishes of his parents, Schneider studied German literature, art history, philosophy, and theatre at the university, all subjects that his family considered inappropriate for a Jew in the German Diaspora. The theatre represented a special refuge in Schneider's imagination as the place from which society can be reformed. Being involved with theatre thus meant for him participating in improving German society and making it more democratic. But once he was working in the theatre, Schneider became aware that he had freely chosen his own ghetto by opting for a career that not only asked him to be "nomadic," but also continues to carry a remnant of the nineteenth-century stigma of the artist as outlaw. And last but not least, Schneider claims that he had to come to terms with another paradox: with its Greek origins, the theatre shows no regard for the Jewish prohibition of pictorial representation.

In his central chapter, "Deutschland," Schneider establishes the link between culture, which is the focus of his previous two chapters, and nationality. Schneider's parents refused to adopt German citizenship until late in the 1970s and lived in Germany as stateless ["heimatlose Ausländer"], a status that made it necessary for them to apply for visas each time they crossed national borders. The main reason for their refusal to adopt German citizenship was that their son could, through an oversight, be drafted into the "Bundeswehr."[37] Schneider states that he had both pragmatic and idealistic motives when, at the age of twenty-three, he decided to become a German citizen. As a foreigner without a homeland, he was not permitted to vote and had to renew his identity card every other year. But the more important reason was that he felt allegiance to the state in which he was born. However, his inner conflict was immense when he picked up his new passport and upon opening it saw the line: "The bearer of this passport is German,"[38] a fact which, as Schneider sardonically reflects, would have made his grandfather turn in his grave had he not risen up in a cloud of smoke over Auschwitz. Schneider concludes this chapter with the observation that life used to be easy for Jews in the preunification FRG on the lee side of Auschwitz. The abnormality of Jewish existence in Germany was reflected in the peculiarity of a Germany divided. However, as Schneider maintains, Jews are forced to "react" in one way or another to growing German nationalism and xenophobia in the wake of unification. But reaction, Schneider contends, is the most telling sign of a failing Diaspora.

In the final two chapters, Richard Chaim Schneider assumes greater distance from his subject matter, his tone becomes more factual, and his appeals to authority outweigh personal anecdotes.

In the chapter entitled "Israel," he discusses the multifaceted relationship between German Jews and Israel and his personal gravitation toward Germany. On the one hand, Israel was exerting worldwide pressure on Jews to leave the Diaspora, especially on German Jews, who in ethical terms rank the lowest on the international Jewish scale because they live in the land where millions of Jews were murdered. On the other hand, in order to cope with the situation in Germany, German Jews have had to keep thinking of Israel as a utopian place. Neither position, according to Schneider, is constructive. He also underscores the cultural differences between Israelis and European Jews: "The spiritual and cultural rift between Diaspora and Israel keeps growing. Israel lies in the Levant … And therefore it becomes increasingly foreign to us European Jews."[39] These differences are aggravated by the fact that those born in Israel do not understand life in the diaspora, which, for Schneider, is a quintessential Jewish experience. Why, he asks, should he as a Jew have to define his "Heimat" geographically? He declares the concept of "Heimat" obsolete in a world of global consciousness and suggests that German Jews define their identity as supranational and commit themselves to a "radical humanism" in accordance with Jewish Law. The dilemma, however, is, according to Schneider, that non-Jewish Germans, in an undemocratic and discriminatory way, keep insisting on the essential difference between German and Jew.

Germany's refusal to become a truly democratic and pluralistic society is, in Schneider's opinion, not the only obstacle to the creation of a "meaningful Diaspora" in Germany. Unlike Jews in other larger diasporic communities in the world, most German Jews neither know Hebrew nor are they familiar with the Torah. However, Judaism will not be able to survive without spiritual practice. The importance Schneider attributes to the study of the Torah is an expression of Jewish self-assertion vis-à-vis non-Jewish Germans and, in particular, the resurgence of anti-Semitism in contemporary Germany. Schneider also blames the institutions of the Central Council of Jews in Germany and above all the "Einheitsgemeinde," the concept of a single official Jewish community for each city, for stifling new spiritual developments and curbing diversity within a particular area.

Last but not least, both Schneider and Lea Fleischmann also write back to the flood of non-Jewish autobiographical texts in response to the Holocaust, a phenomenon that took off in the 1960s and peaked immediately after the national telecast of the American film *Holocaust*.[40] As Jack Zipes points out, "up until the showing of the film *Holocaust* in 1979, German Jews had not made their presence felt in either West or East Germany ... But there had been an unspoken understanding among Jews and between Jews and Germans that it would be best to keep silent and blend in with the rest of the population, not to arouse attention."[41] Both Fleischmann and Schneider, in their own way, demonstrate that breaking this rule is a prerequisite for German Jewish identity and survival.

6 Rewriting Turkey: Barbara Frischmuth and Hanne Mede-Flock

This and the following chapter complement each other in that they both deal with stereotypical views of the "Turk" and of "Turkey" from opposite perspectives. While Austrian writer Barbara Frischmuth and German writer Hanne Mede-Flock critically assess Austrian and German views of Turkey in their novels, Feridun Zaimoglu satirizes the encroachment of Turkish subculture on "German" culture. In this chapter I will demonstrate how Frischmuth's *Das Verschwinden des Schattens in der Sonne* [*The Shadow Disappears in the Sun*] (1973) and Mede-Flock's *Im Schatten der Mondsichel* [*In the Shadow of the Crescent Moon*] (1985)[1] represent their female protagonists' interaction with Turkey as more complex and less "colonizing" than that of the protagonists' of their male predecessors. Yet, despite these two writers' acute awareness of the pitfalls of orientalist discourse, Turkey remains a Eurocentric construct in their texts and, by attempting to undermine some of the cultural stereotypes, Frischmuth and Mede-Flock unwittingly reinforce others.

In *Imperial Eyes: Travel Writing and Transculturation*, Mary Louise Pratt uses the term "seeing man" for the European traveller/travel writer, "who seek[s] to secure [his] innocence in the same moment as [he] assert[s] European hegemony" and "whose imperial eyes passively look out and possess."[2] Although Pratt's discussion focuses on the imperial age, in some postimperial travel writing by European men, particularly about the Islamic Orient, for example, in Elias Canetti's *Die Stimmen von Marrakesch* [*The Voices of Marrakesh*] (1967), the interaction of the narrator with the other culture is still predominantly determined by his colonizing gaze. The orientalism displayed in these texts, although not the reflection of an actual colonial presence, nevertheless shows discursive similarities to the orientalist representations generated by the cultures of imperial powers. The fact that Canetti's title indicates that the auditory is the primary sense of reception is irrelevant in this context since the attitude of the "listening man" in his travelogue is that of the "seeing man" who controls the contact with the other by deciding for himself when to get involved with his surroundings and when to keep his distance.

Rana Kabbani claims that "Canetti is first and foremost on a journey through a host of startling images" that "offer the reader a passage into an Orient that is pure *tableau vivant* in the manner of Flaubert" and that "Morocco for Canetti provides endless images of poverty, disease, sorcery, superstition and sexuality. It is almost as if his eye were searching out the instances of differentness that he could present an audience with, in order to evoke shock, disgust, laughter or pity."[3] The gaze of Canetti's narrator/ autobiographical self, according to Kabbani, is fixed on the Moroccans' cruelty to animals, the repulsiveness of beggars, and the veiled beauty of women. Canetti's narrator establishes his superiority in relationships with the locals not only by exoticizing his surroundings, but also by not disclosing his own ethnic background – he identifies himself as an Englishman – by refusing to learn Arabic and by communicating in French, the language of the colonizer. Furthermore, although he at times chooses not to interfere with local customs out of a misguided sense of propriety [the ill-treatment of the camels], at other times, he feels free to intrude into private space [the house of the family Dahan], and to violate cultural norms [his staring at the unveiled woman]. However, it is not only the narrator's identification with the European colonizer's position that enters into his representation of self. The fact that he is a man also plays a significant role.

Despite the pervasiveness of the orient in German and Austrian literature, little scholarship had been done on orientalism in literature written in German until German critics felt challenged by Edward Said's study of the conceptual production of the orient.

Said claims that "to speak of Orientalism ... is to speak mainly ... of a British and French cultural enterprise,"[4] because other European countries had no colonies in the orient. In his opinion, "the German Orient was almost exclusively a scholarly, or at least a classical, Orient." But he concedes that "what German Orientalism had in common with Anglo-French ... Orientalism was a kind of intellectual *authority* over the Orient within Western culture."[5] Yet, as German critics have recently demonstrated, Germany's and Austria's relationships with the orient have been more complex than Said makes them appear. Donna K. Heizer, for example, explains that although "depictions of the Orient in the history of German literature roughly conform to the kinds of stereotypes described by Said ... different emphases were placed upon these stereotypes at different times ... and because German cultural identities changed over time, different constructions of the Orient were presented in the history of German literature."[6] Turks, in particular, had long been regarded as dangerous neighbours to the east threatening to invade Central Europe. As Heizer points out, in order to defend themselves, Germans and Austrians had "to 'know' their enemy."[7] Therefore it is no coincidence that the first European Department of Oriental Studies was established in Vienna as early as 1754, seventy years after the Austrian Empire escaped Ottoman invasion and forty years before the Ecole Nationale de Langues Orientales Vivantes was founded in Paris.[8]

Two of the more prominent stereotypes of the Middle East in European texts are its depiction as a place of sensuality as well as a place of violence. While both *Verschwinden* and *Mondsichel* avoid stereotyping Turkish men as sexual aggressors, they depict European women as being able to live their sexuality more freely in Turkey than at home. But more importantly, both narratives take place in times of political unrest. Nazire Akbulut assumes that *Verschwinden* uses the 1970 workers' demonstrations in Istanbul and Kocaeli against changes to the Labour Law as a historical backdrop rather than the 1960 Menderes putsch, which occurred while Frischmuth was actually staying in Erzurum as a student.[9] *Mondsichel* seems to take place in the time between the military coups of 1971 and 1980, when the Turkish government attempted to counter the alleged move away from Atatürk's agenda as Muslim fundamentalist, leftist, and Kurdish movements were gaining power.

While Barbara Frischmuth rewrites the traditional *Bildungsro-man* to subvert the Eurocentric assumption underlying much travel literature that the protagonist grows emotionally and spiritually through the encounter with the other culture, Mede-Flock takes the focus away from the individual protagonist and from intellectual life in the city and represents the encounter with Turkey as political. As Arlene Teraoka points out, "while Third World representations by European authors may never be free of Eurocentrism, the cultural biases of the European will appear in different ways, with varying degrees of self-reflection, and within evolving and competing agendas."[10]

The reader learns nothing about the life of Barbara Frischmuth's protagonist prior to her stay in Istanbul. Her identity in the relationships with her Turkish friends is defined solely by the fact that she is a German-speaking student of Oriental Studies who has studied Turkish and who intends to do research for her doctoral thesis about the dervish order of the Bektashi. It is also obvious from the first page of the novel that she will soon return to her home country despite the attempts of some of her friends to talk her into establishing long-term relationships. Although this home country is not identified, the novel suggests that the narrator, like Frischmuth, once herself a student of Oriental Studies, is Austrian. *Verschwinden* leaves it open as to whether or not the narrator is actually going to benefit in the long term from her experiences. Unlike the traditional *Bildungsroman*, this novel does not follow its protagonist back home to depict her reintegration into society.

Because the narrator is Austrian and not German, she constructs Turkey from an Austrian point of view, as is apparent, for example, from her explanation towards the end of the novel that she has changed her views about the Ottoman siege of Vienna. Furthermore, the fact that, unlike Mede-Flock's novel, *Verschwinden* takes place only in Istanbul and only among intellectuals also shapes the protagonist's interaction with Turks in significant ways. Her Turkish friends accept the narrator as intellectually equal because she speaks Turkish – an accomplishment that makes her experience different from that of Canetti's narrator, who does not speak Arabic – and knows more about some aspects of Turkish history, including the history of the Turkish language, than they do. However, in spite of her expertise and historical knowledge, her relationships with both men and women are compromised not only by her being European but, even more so, by her being a woman.

The European woman's freedom of movement is more limited in Middle Eastern societies than that of the "seeing man." Although the narrator shows all the signs of an emancipated "western" woman of the 1970s – she walks the city unaccompanied, smokes and chats with various bookstore owners and has two Turkish lovers – her friends are protective of her. Sevim, who seems like an overbearing older sister, worries when she does not return for dinner and stays up late to make certain that she is safe. Aksu behaves towards her more like a father than a lover, the Tartar gives her maternal advice, and one of the reasons that Turgut follows her about town is to shield her from unpleasant or even violent encounters.

On the other hand, the female narrator is granted relatively intimate contact with the local women from which the "seeing man," for cultural and religious reasons, is excluded. The Tartar discusses her pregnancy with her, and Sevim and Ayten, during an afternoon of clandestine drinking and intimate conversation, pin the narrator to the floor and try to shave her leg and pubic hair with the intention of making her more beautiful,[11] an act that could be interpreted as a rite of passage. Furthermore, the fact that she is a European woman also comes into play in her interaction with strangers and determines expectations and assumptions as well as relations of power. For example, the two women who find her asleep, initiate a conversation and point at their marriage bands and her unringed finger; the school girls to whom she shows Süheyla's photograph wonder why she does not know where to find her; and the mysterious, apparently insane, mosque servant, whom she follows without resistance, almost pushes her over a balustrade. This is as close as the narrator ever comes to having her life threatened in this time of political unrest, curfews, and police violence – ironically within the sanctuary of a mosque. Unlike the "seeing man," whose interaction with the other takes place mainly in public space, that is, in the street, the market, and on the road, Frischmuth's protagonist's interaction with the foreign culture, like that of other women travellers', is circumscribed by her relationship with other people.

But even more characteristic of the woman traveller's/narrator's approach to the foreign culture is her attempt to open herself unconditionally to the foreign surroundings. She longs for a *unio mystica* with the other, a mystical dissolution of her identity, an experience similar to that of the thirty birds in search of the Simurgh, the divine bird, to whom it is eventually revealed that they themselves are the Simurgh, or the illusion of the shadow disappearing in the sun. Thus one of the narrator's greatest fears is to be excluded. She envies Sevim's intimacy with Turgut as much as she wants to be Sevim's confidante. She also has difficulty establishing personal boundaries, so that she sometimes finds the dynamics of this triangular relationship oppressive. The images of the city, which "penetrate" her during her lengthy walks, overwhelm her physically to an extent that by the end of the summer she develops pneumonia and has to be hospitalized.

However, unlike the male protagonist in the typical *Bildungsroman*, Frischmuth's narrator realizes too late how she has failed, and the narrative denies her the opportunity to demonstrate that she has learned from her mistakes. Gudrun Brokoph-Mauch sees the narrator's shortcoming in her inability to ask the right questions. And indeed, toward the end of the novel, the narrator explains that all of a sudden she was overcome by the urge to ask all the questions she had neglected to ask earlier. Brokoph-Mauch's claim also seems to be confirmed by Sevim's criticism of the narrator: "Sometimes I don't understand you, Sevim said. You know us, you live with us, you are interested in everything that affects us, that is, what used to affect us. You speak our language, you know our history, but still, you don't really look around and you fail to see what is going on. You have developed your own view of what still clings to us from the past, but you are not interested in what is new about us."[12] It is only after her almost symbolic near-death experience that the narrator reassesses both her various relationships and her scholarly approach to her dissertation topic – she even decides to abandon her project and write about the present. While the colonizing gaze of Canetti's narrator is turned outward in an attempt to control his immediate surroundings, Frischmuth's narrator is being "controlled" by the outside world because she fails to see.

The narrator's failure to read her surroundings goes hand in hand with her distrust in language. It is this "doubt about language," if not "despair about language,"[13] that links the novel to the Austrian tradition of language scepticism ["Sprachskepsis"] and therefore also to Elias Canetti's *Die Stimmen von Marrakesch*. However, *Verschwinden* differs from Canetti's text in its representation of the orient. While Canetti's narrator dreams of a language reduced to sounds and screams, Frischmuth's protagonist studies the Arabic and Persian roots of modern Turkish as if she were in search of the "Ursprache." But she soon finds out that knowing the history of the language makes it even more difficult for her to communicate: "I was looking at a language as it was changing, but the attempt to keep up with it brought nothing but defeat."[14] She also notices the gulf between written and conversational Turkish: "I had difficulty forming sentences and lapsed into the level of the first weeks when it was hard for me to communicate although I had already read books in the language."[15] When Ersever tells her that two of his writer friends were put in jail, she not only realizes that she lacks the technical vocabulary to discuss legal matters, but she also discovers that she is unfamiliar with Turkey's legal system. And most important, she needs to achieve cultural competence in addition to the ability to form grammatically and idiomatically correct sentences if she is to avoid misunderstandings. Since the narrator has not spent enough time in Turkey to become culturally literate, she fails to read the signs of revolution around her and, above all, Sevim's and Turgut's involvement in it.

The most tragic "misunderstanding," however, is Turgut's violent death. Apparently, Turgut did not participate in the demonstration but was standing by when one of the demonstrators seemed to recognize him and grabbed him by the shoulders. The police, so the narrator believes, interpreted this event as the demonstrators' attack on the passers-by and reacted by shooting into the crowd, killing Turgut and two others. The fact that the novel concludes with the image of the white body of a man whose skin is marked by a bleeding black hole where the bullet entered, and not on the protagonist's "happy" return to Austria, can be read as the refusal to comply in this novel with the rules of the traditional *Bildungsroman*. However, the conclusion also represents Turkey as a place in which violence may erupt indiscriminately and, at least to "western" eyes, unpredictably.

While *Verschwinden* deals with the individual's failure to find a satisfying way of approaching the other, Hanne Mede-Flock's *Im Schatten der Mondsichel* shifts the focus from the individual to a group of protagonists. Judith, one of the main characters, is a German who quits her job in a travel agency and leaves her husband to work in an Istanbul hospital. Her colleague and friend Berrin, daughter of a Turkish mother and a German father, teaches her Turkish and, inspired by Judith's fascination with Turkey, follows her to Istanbul where she ends up working as a journalist for an underground newspaper. Mehmet, Schaban, and his brother-in-law Alparslan leave Yesilçay, which is wiped out shortly after by the military, to find work and political action in Istanbul. While the novel caricatures these three (and other) male characters, it portrays the female characters Judith, Berrin, Nilüfer (the medical student turned bourgeois housewife), Dr. Kahraman (the lesbian senior medical officer), the intellectual Aysche, and the illiterate Schengül as both individuals and representatives of women in different walks of life. The novel therefore offers a political analysis of women's oppression in a patriarchal society and, by analogy, of the betrayal of the Turks by those western nations that turn a blind eye to the Turkish government's violation of human rights and supply it with arms to fight the Kurds and political dissidents.

Unlike in *Verschwinden*, where the protagonist's Austrian background is not used for contrastive observations about the two cultures, in *Mondsichel* Judith's and Berrin's German background gives rise to cultural comparisons. Judith leaves Germany to escape from a world which she associates with "consumer society, salary increases, profit rates, daily routine and alienated work."[16] Turkish hospitality and compassion are contrasted with German indifference and emotional coldness. Dr. Kahraman, who believes that people who suppress their emotions will fall ill, explains to Judith that her chronic hepatitis can be interpreted as her body's reaction to a repressive environment, that is, an insensitive husband and a society that does not meet her emotional needs. Listening to Judith's life story, Dr. Kahraman wonders whether Judith's husband is one of those Germans who are in favour of political measures to encourage guest workers to return to their home countries because they believe that they take away jobs from the Germans.

Mede-Flock creates in Judith a European traveller whose behaviour contrasts in significant ways with that of Frischmuth's protagonist. Judith quickly decides that book knowledge is not going to be useful in her encounter with the locals in Anatolia: "Of all things, a Goethe quotation popped into her head whose content was not at all relevant to the situation, like everything else she had read about Turkey."[17] Judith's approach to the other culture is characterized by action and involvement. Unlike Frischmuth's protagonist, who after two futile attempts to contact Süheyla, loses interest and gives up, Judith eventually manages to deliver a message to Mehmet after following him across Anatolia and Kurdistan. Judith also witnesses the government troops' attack on Yesilçai. When she describes the atrocities to Berrin and expresses difficulty in coping with what she has seen, Berrin responds with a lecture that sounds similar to and yet quite different from the one Sevim gives Frischmuth's protagonist: "'I don't understand one thing,' said Berrin, 'you travel to Turkey almost every year for two or three months. You have seen much and you know the opinions of your friends about their country's political situation. That should be enough to help you cope with the events in Yesilçai.'"[18] The textual similarity between this passage and that in Frischmuth's novel quoted above, in addition to other intertextual analogies, leads me to believe that Mede-Flock was familiar with Frischmuth's novel and might actually be responding to it. If one compares Berrin's assessment of Judith with Sevim's criticism of Frischmuth's protagonist, it is obvious that Judith, because of her involvement, is able to narrow the cultural gap, whereas Frischmuth's protagonist is not. While both women's bodies react to the foreign environment with illness, Judith's hepatitis, as mentioned above, is explained as a reaction to the familiar, that is, Germany, rather than the unfamiliar Turkey. And last but not least, when Judith decides to spend the night with the owner of the movie theatre from the next village rather than in the company of her new friend Nilüfer and the other women, her immediate response when the women shun her is to judge them as intolerant and indoctrinated with male standards. However, she soon realizes that she should at least have openly discussed with the women the cultural differences between western and eastern sexual behaviour. Frischmuth's protagonist, on the other hand, hides from Sevim the fact that she spent the night with Turgut, and the gulf between the two women consequently widens.

Although one part of *Mondsichel* focuses on the relationship of the six women and their male partners during the time they are living together in Istanbul, Anatolia and Kurdistan play important roles in the novel as the places of origin and/or destination of most of the characters. Anatolia is home to the families of Mehmet, Schaban, Schengül, and Alparslan, and at the end of the novel Schaban and his young daughter Hafize return to Yesilçai. Mehmet, who left Istanbul to teach in Bursa, loses his teaching license as soon as the government learns about his political activity and founds an agricultural commune in Söke together with other teachers who share his lot. And Dr. Kahraman leaves Istanbul at the end of a life-long career in order to offer medical expertise to the poor and needy in Kurdistan. The novel thus moves in a circle from the country to the city and back to the country. It opens with a description of village life in Anatolia where Judith is shown interacting with the locals. The peasants' life is represented as one of extreme hardship and brutal exploitation by the agas. When Judith, in search of Mehmet, arrives in Diyarbakir, she observes that the conditions in which people live here are even worse than those in Anatolia. Both of these rural areas are depicted as being ruled by Islamic fundamentalist leaders, and life in the two villages is characterized by the oppression of women and children.

If Mede-Flock is guilty of stereotypical representation, it is for her one-sided depiction of rural Turkish women as victims of patriarchy. As Marilya Veteto-Conrad points out in citing the sociologist Serim Timur, "contrary to common Western belief, patriarchal family units constitute only one-fourth to one-fifth of [Turkish] villages and small towns."[19] Veteto-Conrad concludes that "Germans, for whom the socio-cultural system of Turkish male and female roles is close to incomprehensible, cannot see beyond the image of the harem as a symbol for Turkish norms"[20] and that even Turkish-born women writers in Germany sometimes perpetuate the stereotype of the Turkish woman as victim. Aysel Özakin, for example, reinforces the western stereotype of the Turkish woman as exploited and oppressed by Turkish men in her novel Die Preisvergabe [The Prizegiving] (1979).[21] Mede-Flock, however, manages to balance her critical representation of the victim status of rural women by showing that victimization of women is ubiquitous and by depicting her female characters as capable of initiating change.

In Mondsichel, the patriarchal structures found in the country do not lose their temporary power over the female characters living in the city. This is obvious from the way Alparslan and even the revolutionary Mehmet treat their wives. Istanbul is the place, however, where all the characters, with the exception of Alparslan, eventually experience some kind of transformation. And, as mentioned above, some of them return to the country with the intention of bringing about social change, a development that seems to indicate hope for the future of rural Turkey. However, this change, the novel implies, is unlikely to be brought about by government intervention and can only be accomplished through the personal involvement and initiative of the educated.

Within the context of *Mondsichel*, to be educated is not synonymous with being intellectual. Rather, it is a state of social awareness and compassion which is opposed to the mystical and apolitical "dissolution of the self" that Frischmuth's protagonist is seeking. Women, who for Mede-Flock play the most important part in social and political progress, have first to learn how to free themselves from various societal restraints before they can achieve self-fulfillment. The three women in *Mondsichel* who most conspicuously infringe upon male-defined conventions, Dr. Kahraman, Judith, and Berrin, are censored accordingly by the men with whom they have contact. Dr. Kahraman becomes the subject of homophobic slurs when the two male nurses watch her engrossed in a discussion of a patient with Nilüfer. However, the text does not grant the men the power to confront Dr. Kahraman openly. They only dare to talk about her behind her back. Judith is likewise censored indirectly rather than directly. When she asks one of the high officials in Diyarbakir for information about Mehmet, the traveller's unconventional behaviour and appearance seem to offend him personally: "The gentleman was taken aback and he turned away discreetly. He had pictured a European lady somewhat differently. He had not at all expected to be confronted with an obstinate creature with muscular arms and legs, whose loose bleached hair looked as disheveled as the mane of the horse."[22] Berrin, however, to whom Akbulut refers as an "idealized feminist" is, because of her literacy in both cultures, the most self-confident and independent among the younger women. She challenges male domination effectively and reduces the male characters' interaction with her to compliance and disgruntled scowls.

Female solidarity manifests itself in the women's emotional and practical support of each other and of other victims of the system. Dr. Kahraman and Nilüfer, for example, who disapprove of

Mehmet's selling Aysche's poetry as his own, find a publisher for her work so that she finally receives the recognition she deserves. Berrin and Dr. Kahraman help Nilüfer to leave a marriage that offers her security but nothing else and facilitate her return to the medical profession. When Schengül kills Alparslan in self-defence, Dr. Kahraman and her lawyer friend Nihal dispose of the body and protect Schengül from both the corrupt legal system and suspicious family members. The women also bring about Schaban's release from prison, where he was awaiting the death penalty for a burglary which he did not commit, and found an organization to fight for the rights of women and political prisoners.

While the female characters' political strategies are characterized by ingenuity, humour, and courage, those of the male characters are defined by inflexibility, violence, and cowardice. Self-gratification, for example, overrules the interest of the community in Mehmet's and Schaban's actions. As Nazire Akbulut points out, Mehmet's murder of a political opponent is thus contrasted with Schengül's murder of her husband: "While the horridness of Mehmet's murder is depicted in realistic detail, the narrator resorts to myth to describe Schengül's deed."[23] The crescent moon casts its shadow as Schengül picks up the axe, which is mythically transformed into a labrys, and she reclaims her own life and that of other women. In matriarchal mythology the moon presages change and brings life during its crescent phase. By foregrounding the feminine principle of the crescent moon, the text eclipses its meaning as the emblem adopted by the Ottoman Empire. According to *The Woman's Dictionary of Symbols and Sacred Objects*, "so important was the Moon Goddess in pre-Islamic Arabia that her emblem came to represent the entire country, and still does so, as the lunar crescent on Islamic flags. As Manat, the old Moon-mother of Mecca, she once ruled the fates of all her sons, who also called her Al-Lat, the Goddess. Now she has been masculinized into 'Allah,' who forbids women to enter the shrines that were once founded by priestesses of the Moon."[24] In Mede-Flock's visual pun, the crescent moon's shadow can therefore be interpreted as women's oppression by state and religion, an oppression they have to overcome through collaborative efforts.

The image of the crescent moon casting its shadow also contrasts with that of the disappearance of the shadow in the sun in Frischmuth's novel. While the sun represents male energy and the image of the disappearance of the sun is based on male mythology, as it is taken from a tale in Farudeddin Attar's *The Book of Birds*, *Mondsichel* resorts to matriarchal mythology, just as Frischmuth reconstructs women's history and redefines their position in society in her subsequent novels *Die Mystifikationen der Sophie Silber* [*The Mystifications of Sophie Silber*] (1976), and *Amy oder die Metamorphose* [*Amy or the Metamorphosis*] (1978), and in her play *Die Frau im Mond* [*The Woman in the Moon*] (1982).

While *Verschwinden* focuses on the protagonist's failure to comprehend the other culture despite her book knowledge about it, *Mondsichel* projects an almost utopian view of the possibility of overcoming cultural barriers through solidarity and political action. Turkey is attractive to Frischmuth's narrator – just as is Morocco to Canetti's – because it remains incomprehensible. As Georg Pichler points out, the protagonist's lack of self-knowledge in *Verschwinden* is partly responsible for her failure.[25] *Mondsichel* focuses on a variety of characters who all have different backgrounds as regards nationality, culture, class, gender, and sexual orientation, in order to show how identity is historically and socially shaped by these factors. *Verschwinden* does not follow the protagonist back to Austria, whereas *Mondsichel* reunites Judith and Berrin in Germany where they accidentally meet during a demonstration against the completion of the nuclear plant in Brokdorf. Both have learned from their life in Turkey that political action does not stop at national borders.

To arrive at a fair assessment of the two novels and their representation of Turkey, one needs to read them against the cultural and personal backgrounds of their authors and the political and historical contexts that inform their writing. While Frischmuth's text is an early response to male travel writing about the orient such as *Die Stimmen von Marrakesch* and implicitly contrasts female and male modes of interaction with the other, Mede-Flock's text can be read as a response to novels like *Verschwinden*, which from a feminist point of view might seem apolitical and esoteric. *Verschwinden* evokes stereotypical images of Austria as a peaceful country that provides neither the space nor need for political action and therefore fails to prepare the protagonist for her stay in Turkey, a country represented as haunted by violence. By contrast, Mede-Flock depicts the clashes between demonstrators and police in Germany as almost as violent as those in Turkey. By dedicating the novel to Nuriye Bekir, who was stabbed by her husband in front of a women's shelter in Berlin while her four children looked on, Mede-Flock draws attention to the fact that, with the arrival of Turkish migrants in Germany and a growing Turkish German population, Turkey has moved closer to Germany than Germans ever thought possible. This new reality, so the novel suggests, requires that Germans and Turks learn from each other. Feridun Zaimoglu, however, whose texts I discuss in the following chapter, undermines such liberal discourse.

7 Writing Back to Liberal Discourse: Feridun Zaimoglu's Grotesque Realism

While José F.A. Oliver and Zehra Çirak question the "normalcy" of the dominant culture in their poetry rather than dwell on their own status as other, Feridun Zaimoglu creates an alternative identity that refuses to define itself as part of a homogenous ethnic group. Instead, it sees itself connected to a transnational "ethnic" consciousness. *Enfant terrible* of the contemporary German literary scene, Zaimoglu[1] has set out to save German migrant writing from the stigma of being "lachrymose, sycophantic, and publicly subsidized"[2] "Gastarbeiterliteratur" that casts the migrant in the role of the perpetual victim. He argues that the often discussed identity crisis of second-generation Turks in Germany was invented by mainstream media and publishers. Adopting the term "Kanake," a discriminatory term for Turks and those considered to look "Turkish," for the "new" generation of "Turks," he claims in the introduction to *Kanak Sprak* that "Kanaken do not seek cultural moorings. Neither do they want to shop in the identity supermarket nor merge into the egalitarian herd of refugees. They have internalized their own values, and they insist on self-definition. They are the generation X proper, having been denied individuation as well as ontogenesis."[3] Zaimoglu insists that the Turkish minority in Germany is not what the Germans believe it to be.

Günter Wallraff's undercover reportage *Ganz Unten* [*At the Bottom*] (1985), in which he meant to uncover the exploitation of

Turkish workers, has significantly contributed to reifying the image of the "Turk" in German popular and political discourse as inferior, illiterate, and oppressed. *Ganz Unten* immediately climbed up the German bestseller list and was soon translated into several European languages. The German-language edition alone sold almost three million copies.[4] To write this book, journalist Günter Wallraff "cross-dressed" as a Turk by wearing dark contact lenses and a dark hairpiece and by speaking "Ausländerdeutsch." Wallraff maintains that pretending to be naïve and uneducated made it easier for him to unmask bigotry and xenophobia: "Playing the fool made me smarter and gave me an insight into the narrow-mindedness and coldness of a society that thinks of itself as so intelligent, superior, authoritative, and just. I was the fool whom people openly told the truth."[5] Disguised as "Ali" and with the help of a hidden tape recorder and video camera, Wallraff set out to unveil the inhuman and illegal conditions under which many migrants in Germany were forced to work in the 1960s and 1970s.

Although Günter Wallraff deserves credit to a certain extent for having increased the average German's awareness of the alarming degree of xenophobia in German society, his critics agree that *Ganz Unten* confirmed the stereotype of the "Turk" as someone who picks up the dirty work that no one else is willing to do. This assumption was already reflected in the wording of the newspaper advertisement with which Wallraff launched his masquerade: "Foreigner, strong, looking for work, no matter what, heavy or dirty work ok, also for little money."[6] The flaw in Wallraff's method is the self-fulfillingly prophetic potential of such wording. Someone who advertises himself as being prepared to do dirty work will probably be asked to do just that.

Günter Wallraff's assumption that foreigners in Germany are a homogenous group of illiterate and exploited workers also provoked the criticism of Turkish intellectuals like Aysel Özakin, who explains that she wanted to leave the Federal Republic when she first saw *Ganz Unten* displayed in a bookstore window. She points out that the sullen, despondent, dirty face [i.e. Wallraff's in his masquerade] on the cover of the book drove her into an identity crisis.[7] Why, Özakin asks herself, did she suddenly feel compelled to identify with each and every Turk she saw in the street? In "Ali hinter den Spiegeln," she deplores both the "German" tendency to think of others in terms of national rather than individual identity and the concomitant phenomenon of reducing the role of "third-world" writers to spokespersons with an obligation to bemoan the oppression of "their" people. Consequently, Özakin argues, individuality and avantgardism remain privileges of intellectuals in the countries of Western Europe."[8]

A decade later Feridun Zaimoglu, who, unlike Aysel Özakin, grew up in the Federal Republic, has been able to treat the reification of "Ali" in a more playful and satirical manner and to claim these privileges for himself. In *Kanak Sprak* and *Abschaum* Zaimoglu parodies Wallraff's narrative strategies and satirizes at least four of his premises: The "Turk" is unable to speak idiomatically and grammatically correct German, the "Turk" is at the bottom, the "Turk" is male, and the "Turk" is unable to voice his own opposition to exploitation. These assumptions, on which Wallraff based his project, also imply that he believed in his capacity for unbiased and disinterested observation, and that he must have been convinced that his act of cross-dressing was the only means of authenticating German xenophobia. In addition, he must have thought of himself not only as having access to "the truth" but also as being able to interpret this truth "correctly": "Sure, I wasn't really a Turk. But one has to disguise oneself to unmask society; one must deceive and play a part to discover the truth."[9]

The fact that parts of *Ganz Unten* seem to have been ghostwritten and that Wallraff ascribed experiences of his Turkish coworkers to "Ali,"[10] adds to the ethical dilemma of this ethnojournalistic experiment. However, contrary to what Wallraff believes, an experiment, that is, an act that can be replicated, ultimately lacks subversive potential. In an interview, Wallraff naively claims that the liberating force of the book emanates from the Ali figure, as he calls the alleged guest worker, who "rakes the muck, does not consent, and refuses to swallow everything."[11] Wallraff continues his description of Ali, switching to the pronoun "I" when referring to him: "I don't just take it. I also give back. This is the potential of resistance from below."[12] By confusing the literary character Ali, who, so Wallraff believes, lends the book its "liberating force" and is "the secret to its success," with the reality of a guest worker and furthermore with his own privileged position, Wallraff robs his book of exactly that oppositional force.

Although Günter Wallraff claims to have adopted the masquerade as a political strategy to help the oppressed and thus as a form of social critique, he also admits to having had selfish motives. Adopting the role of Ali gave him the freedom to explore his own identity: "To live inside the role is at the same time a game, a completely liberating element, more intense and authentic. For me it is again and again a search for identity, an opportunity to find myself, and my curiosity is also involved."[13] The degree to which Wallraff's experiment was a performative act is particularly obvious from the way in which he resolved the language barrier, that is, his inability to speak Turkish. At first, he pretended to be a deaf mute and asked a Turk, who played his brother, to act as his interpreter. But, this strategy undermined his intention of drawing the truth out of both his Turkish and his German interlocutors. He then claimed political reasons for refusing to speak his alleged mother tongue, namely as a protest against the violation of human rights in Turkey. To many of his Turkish coworkers, however, this form of protest seemed exaggerated. Wallraff points out that the fact that the German of many of the younger workers was better than their Turkish and because he usually worked in a group of colleagues of various nationalities, the risk of being found out by his Turkish coworkers was diminished. To produce the "Ausländerdeutsch" in which he finally decided to communicate, he randomly dropped grammatical endings, shifted parts of the sentence, and often simply spoke in a broken version of the Cologne dialect.

To counter the image of the "Turk" as someone who relies on pidgin German to communicate with the Germans, Feridun Zaimoglu creates the figure of the *Kanake* who draws his identity from an insider language, a German of his own creation. *Kanaken*, or *Kanakstas*,[14] speak a language that is based on underground vocabulary and has its own rhythm: "'Kanak-Sprak,' a kind of creole or thieves' argot with secret codes and signs. Their language is related to the free-style recitation of rap. Both are first and foremost an attitude."[15] In forging their own language, *Kanaken* have developed a transnational consciousness comparable to that cultivated by the Black power movement. The *Kanake* refuses to assimilate; his culture is a subculture operating on the margins of society.

Feridun Zaimoglu's first book, *Kanak Sprak*, poses as a collection of twenty-four short autobiographical pieces that the author/narrator/ethnographer purports to have derived from taped conversations. With this strategy, Zaimoglu parodies Wallraff's claim of authenticity. His native informants are rappers, a transsexual, workers, pimps, petty thieves, sex trade workers, junkies, a poet called Memet, and an Islamist. Zaimoglu maintains that what unites these men is the fact that they are all members of a minority. However, it is immediately obvious that these texts are not unrehearsed first-person chronicles. Zaimoglu's characters are caricatures who embody the stereotypes associated with "Turks." To undermine these stereotypes, Zaimoglu explodes the mainstream media's representation of the "Turk." This strategy of exaggerating the media image to undermine it has been employed by African American rap groups as a powerful means of social criticism. Zaimoglu adopts the conventions of the street ethnography of Gangsta Rap, a genre depicting the activities of lawless black urban gangs. Gangsta Rap lyrics have no claim to authenticity and objectivity, but, as Michael Quinn points out, "rather than questioning or denying the veracity of mainstream representations of life in inner cities, Gangsta Rap accepts the gang member – drug seller role assigned to urban black youth by the media and then hyperbolizes these representations until the rappers become exactly what whites fear."[16] By appropriating notions of criminality for black identity, rappers turn delinquency into a metaphor for power. Similarly, Zaimoglu depicts *Kanaksta* involvement with drugs, prostitution, and theft to signify self-identification and liberation from "German" attempts to contain the image of the "Turk."

In the 1980s, Germany developed its own hip-hop and rap culture with unique traditions and themes. Cora E., the *grande dame* of German rap music, as Christoph Ribbat refers to her, admits to having been inspired by African American rap without, however, imitating or adopting its language and lyrics.[17] She explains that she raps about what is familiar to her and that, as she has not experienced racism, she does not rap about it. One of the greatest successes has been her song "Schlüsselkind" ["Latchkey Kid"], whose first line "I come from the middle class" expresses her nonidentification with deprivileged urban youth. Cora E., together with Die Fantastischen 4, the German rap group that has paved the way for others like it, have succeeded in establishing a German rap tradition. Over the last few years, several rap bands, whose members are of Turkish, Italian, Yugoslav, Arab, or Asian descent, have also conquered the German rap scene. Groups such as Advanced Chemistry, Cartel, Fresh Familee, Sons of Gastarbeita, Cribb 199, and Da Crime Posse have all been successful. The lyrics of the songs of these groups obviously draw on the lyrics of the songs of their African American counterparts. As one band member of Sons of Gastarbeita puts it, "Of course life is a lot tougher in the U.S. ghettos. But there are parallels between Black Americans and young foreigners in Germany."[18] The Sons of Gastarbeita, for example, perceive their music as "creative rebellion" against the discrimination to which second and third-generation Turks are exposed on a daily basis. In their lyrics as well as during stage performances, they parody the German stereotypes associated with the Arabic and Turkish backgrounds of their group members by donning veils, singing about Arabian Nights, and parodying Turkish jokes, which are a common currency in Germany.[19]

Not surprisingly, two of the "native informants" in *Kanak Sprak* are rappers. Abdurrahman in the first of the twenty-four pseudoautobiographical pieces, entitled "Pop is ne fatale Orgie" ["Pop Sucks"], contrasts pop and rap as musical styles in a way comparable to that in which Feridun Zaimoglu situates guest worker literature and *Kanak* "ethnography" at opposite ends of the spectrum of writing. For Abdurrahman, pop is flat, sentimental, and inauthentic just as guest worker literature is for Zaimoglu. In "Der direkte Draht zum schwarzen Mann" ["The direct line to the black man"] Ali, another rapper, is a disciple of Chuck D, leader of the group Public Enemy. Chuck D's lyrics, "delivered in a charismatic, booming baritone, are almost exclusively pro-Black history lessons. Public Enemy was the first rap group to focus the music's potential on social change."[20] Ali explains that in the same way the members of Da Crime Posse, one of Germany's most popular "gangster rap" groups, attempt to lure teenagers away from the gang and drug scene by appealing to them with empowering rap messages. According to Ali, rap offers the young a valid alternative to both assimilation and ghettoization. As in the African American nationalist movement, the autonomy of the community and the construction of a self-defined identity become the primary goals for the *Kanakstas*.

The "direct line to the black man" is evoked in several of the ethnographic pieces. The drug dealer Akay, for example, maintains: "We are all niggers here. We have our ghetto. We carry it with us wherever we go. We steam foreign. Our sweat is nigger. Our life is nigger. The gold chains are nigger. Our big noses and mugs and our style are so bloody nigger that we scratch our skin like crazy and by doing so we understand that it is not the old black skin that makes the nigger but being different and living a different lifestyle."[21] As much as Zaimoglu's *Kanakstas* identify with African Americans, they voice their contempt for those who sell out to the dominant culture and attempt to "pass," that is, strive to live the middle-class life of their German neighbours.

While *Kanak Sprak* aspires to embrace the whole spectrum of "*Lumpenethnier*," another term Feridun Zaimoglu uses to refer to the *Kanakstas*, Zaimoglu's second book *Abschaum*, which purports to tell the "true story of Ertan Ongun," is set exclusively in the drug and sex trade milieu. In *Abschaum*, as in *Kanak Sprak*, the author/editor functions as a mediator between the native informant, in this case a twenty-five-year-old *Kanaksta*, and the reader. In the afterword to the text, Zaimoglu claims tongue in cheek that after having read *Kanak Sprak* and having been impressed by its audacity and authenticity, Ertan Ongun felt encouraged to approach him with the words: "I will give you pure stuff. You are my dealer. Go and sell it!"[22]

Obviously rap musicians are not the first and only ones to use the rhetoric of the outcast. Artaud, Brecht, Genet, Pasolini, and Tarantino, among many others, come to mind. Their common forebear is Rabelais, from whose writing Mikhail Bakhtin developed the concepts of carnival and the grotesque body. For Bakhtin, the grotesque body is representative of the empowering forces of popular culture that enable it to undermine and subvert official culture. He describes this marketplace culture as nonprivatized and communal. Analogously, most of the episodes narrated in *Kanak Sprak* and *Abschaum* take place in the street, in the flea market, in seedy bars, in brothels, and in jail. These spaces are to be understood both literally and metaphorically. Zaimoglu's "Turk" lives in the space between various cultures and is both physically and spiritually homeless. In Zaimoglu's texts, the flea market, the discotheque, the prison, and the brothel are the offspring of Rabelais' marketplace. The brothel, as one of the "Turk's" places of refuge, exaggerates the German stereotype of the sexual prowess of Turkish men and the common equation of Turk and pimp. The trope of the prison signals imprisonment by the prevailing stereotypes associated with "Turks" in German society and their reification by authors like Günter Wallraff as well as by self-hatred. Lack of self-respect, reinforced by a society that treats the "Turk" as a criminal and parasite, creates the "grotesque body" of the "Turk." As the poet Memet sums it up in "Die Beschmutzten kennen keine Ästhetik" ["The Soiled Have No Aesthetics"]:

We want to adorn ourselves with the insignia of the blond supermen. Our own bad taste undermines us as well as the feelings of inferiority instilled in us. That is why many Turkish mamas dye their hair blond and our pop starlets wear blue or green contacts. That is why the Turk kid covets the Daimler. That is why many a Turk uses his knife: He wants to be hard as Krupp steel and look like a tough guy. We have not digested the shift from fieldwork to conveyor belt ... As long as this country refuses us real entrance, we will absorb the anomalies and perversities of this country like a sponge and spit out the muck. The soiled know nothing of aesthetics.[23]

According to Bakhtin, "the [grotesque] body swallows the world and is itself swallowed by the world,"[24] its focus being on the mouth, the anus, and the phallus. The grotesque image of the body and the focus on the "material bodily stratum" is captured in the "language of the marketplace," that is, a scatological language characterized by exaggeration and hyperbole.[25] Likewise, caricature of the "Turk" and inflation of his oppression are trademarks of Zaimoglu's writing. The language of the *Kanaksta* is, as discussed above, a substandard sociolect, replete with scatology and images meant to shock the mainstream reader. Ertan Ongun, Zaimoglu's "native informant" in *Abschaum* concludes his street ethnography with the following statement: "I'm sitting here now and try to shock our intellectuals. I try to scare our assimilated and to fascinate certain people: Fascination for the criminal subject, fascination for the wild Other, fascination for those who are at the bottom."[26] Apart from echoing the title of Wallraff's book, Ertan Ongun's statement of the purpose of his text satirizes Günter Wallraff's claim to be both truthful and subversive as well as his fascination for the "Other" at the bottom.

When the poet Memet, who can be taken as Zaimoglu's mouth-
piece, blames Germany for "refusing entrance" to this "other,"
that is, refusing to give guest workers and their children citizenship rights, he also points at the consequences of such politics.
The unwanted "others" will accept the "anomalies and perversities" of their host country and spit out what they cannot swallow.

In "Gangsta Culture – Sexism, Misogyny: Who Will Take the
Rap?," bell hooks argues that "gangsta rap … is not a product
created in isolation within a segregated black world but is rather
expressive of the cultural crossing, mixings, and engagement of
black youth culture with the values, attitudes, and concerns of the
white majority."[27] She emphasizes that it is the application of
mainstream cultural values, "largely learned through passive,
uncritical consumption of the mass media, that is most revealed
in gangsta rap."[28] What applies to the street culture of black youth
also applies to the street culture of young Turks in Germany. The
absence of positive male role models within their "own" culture
and the degrading image of Ali that is projected on them by the
mainstream media, trigger identity crisis, violence, misogyny, and
self-destructive behaviour such as drug addiction.

In Rabelaisian grotesque realism the expression "at the bottom,"
as referring to social status, also takes on the meaning of the
"lower part of the body," that is, the genital organs and the
buttocks. Ali, who is perceived as being at the bottom, is transformed into the *Kanaksta* whose interaction with the outside world
is defined by his lower body. "Die Arschlochfoto-Story" ["The
Asshole Photo Story"] in *Abschaum* gives an example of Zaimoglu's
use of the "material body lower stratum," as defined by Bakhtin,
to create his own brand of grotesque realism with the intention
of writing back to both bourgeois realism and the realism of
"Literatur der Betroffenheit." The narrator and his friend Kemal,
both heavily drugged, are passing the evening in a discotheque.
Two blond Polish women, who would like to dance, ask the two
men if they would watch their camera while they are on the dance
floor. The narrator and his friend go to the washroom where he
takes a picture of Kemal's penis and Kemal takes a picture of the
narrator's anus. Returning from Poland, where they had the film
developed and were asked embarrassing questions about the pictures, the two women confront the narrator and want to know if

and why he and his friend took the pictures. When the narrator realizes that the women do not believe he is innocent, he claims that what they see in the pictures is his penis and his friend's anus. His shoes, however, give him away. The women hand him the pictures, and he hangs his "asshole photo" on his apartment wall. When people ask him if he took a picture of his "asshole," the narrator replies: "I took a picture of my asshole and hung it because I find it cool."[29]

This story describes a reality about which the average reader does not care to read, but as much as the story attempts to portray the reality of a section of the German population, it also plays with clichés and undermines reader expectations. The fact that the two "Turks" are too drugged to be interested in picking up the women, for example, undermines the stereotype of the oversexed "Turkish" male who is particularly attracted to blond women. That the two women are Polish and therefore outsiders in German society makes the story more realistic, in that it is easier for people of different nationalities to meet socially than it is for Turks to meet Germans. As Zaimoglu points out in an interview with Joachim Lottman, many Turkish men in Germany have Polish partners. The fact that the Polish women are afraid that someone might steal their camera, however, makes fun of the stereotype of Poland as a nation of thieves. The provocative pictures being developed in "Catholic" Poland also contributes to the humour of the story. The women's ability to identify the narrator in the picture by his shoes serves as comic relief, but it can also be read as a sarcastic comment on what defines the "Turk." Hanging the picture on the wall is obviously an act of defiance. However, it also provides an example of how the "anomalies and perversities" of mainstream culture, as the poet Memet puts it, are recycled.

The world that Zaimoglu portrays is, as in African American rap, a man's world, and the behaviour of his characters is extremely misogynistic. While texts by Turkish German women writers often express both the victimization of Turkish women and their strength either to endure or rebel against male dominance, Turkish grandmothers, mothers, and sisters are absent from Zaimoglu's texts. The women depicted in the two texts that I discuss in this chapter are prostitutes.[30] When one reads Joachim Lottmann's interview with Feridun Zaimoglu, one gains the impression that for him the definition of *Kanaksta* identity includes a confirmation of their virility. How much of his endorsement of "Turkish" machismo – he talks about *Kanakstas* racing each other in big German cars on the *autobahn* and spending much of their time at boxing matches – is meant to be taken seriously or is said tongue in cheek is difficult to tell.

The *Kanaksta's* need to reassert a new "manhood" that distinguishes itself from that of the older generation, as well as the attempt to create a new migrant discourse, remind me of Frank Chin's crusade against both the mainstream media and Chinese American women writers. Frank Chin, a well-known writer, self-styled "Chinatown Cowboy," and one of the most outspoken revisionists of Chinese American history, has attacked Maxine Hong Kingston and Amy Tan for falsifying Chinese and Chinese American history in their novels and creating a distorted image of Chinese men. According to Chin, "rampant Chinese misogyny is a bum rap, a product of white Christian imagination, not history."[31] The impetus to reassert manhood also underlies the attempt of Chin and other male Chinese American writers to recover a heroic literary tradition of their own. Chin condemns autobiography and the expression of personal pain in the writing by Chinese American women to the same extent that Zaimoglu condemns what he calls "lachrymose and sycophantic" guest worker literature. Furthermore, Chin has also criticized Kingston, Tan, and other Chinese American women writers, for taking their white readers on a Chinatown tour, that is, catering to white readers by explaining "Chinese" traditions to them. Some of the Turkish German women writers like Saliha Scheinhard and even Renan Demirkan could be found guilty of catering in a similar manner to the German reader. In contrast, Zaimoglu, like Chin, intends to undermine the dominant culture's reading expectations by being provocative and "politically incorrect." Rewriting is the writer's most effective strategy of demonstrating a revisionist stance. Thus, in *The Chinaman Pacific & Frisco R.R. Co.*, Frank Chin, in a satirical manner, writes back to Maxine Hong Kingston's *The Woman Warrior* to counter her alleged feminization of Chinese American men and her alleged falsification of Chinese history. To show how far removed Günter Wallraff is from telling the "truth," in *Ganz Unten*, Feridun Zaimoglu writes back to the "realistic" account of Ali's dialogue with the owner of a funeral parlour in his "grotesquely realistic" "Die Beerdigungs-Story" ["The Burial Story"].

Pretending that he has only two months to live, Ali visits a funeral parlour in a wheelchair to choose a coffin and arrange for its transportation to Turkey. Wallraff complains that the owner of the parlour, whom he describes as a callous business woman, failed to show any compassion when he told her that he was dying of lung cancer as a result of working with asbestos. Wallraff expresses his dismay that the woman asked him questions neither about the nature of his work nor about the nature of his medical treatment. Granted, some of the exchanges between Ali and the woman sound macabre because she is, in order to accommodate this customer's particular wishes, anticipating his death, so to speak. However ethically unsound too keen a sense of business may be when one is dealing with a dying person, pretending to be dying to seek someone's compassion seems no less unethical. Furthermore, Wallraff draws the dubious conclusion from this experience that even on his deathbed Ali is being exploited and treated as an object. "Buried alive among the living," as Wallraff puts it, Ali is "taking refuge among the dead."

In "Die Beerdigungs-Story," Feridun Zaimoglu has his narrator take care of a friend's burial arrangements. As it took some time to determine the cause of death – the German authorities suspected foul play – the corpse is already badly decomposed. By Islamic law, it must be washed before it can be buried, so the narrator offers to help with the procedure. He does not spare the reader a detailed description of the rotting corpse's state of decomposition, giving precise details about odour, colour, and texture. The repulsiveness of these details overpowers any other sentiment both in the experience of the narrator as well as in that of the reader. In contrast to Wallraff's dubious attempt to unmask the "ugliness" of treating a dying "Turk" as if he were already dead, Zaimoglu describes the "ugliness" of "Ali's" dead body. Again, as in "Die Arschlochfoto-Story" the "Turk" is being metonymically reduced to anus and stinking corpse respectively. This corpse is not the first depicted in Turkish German literature. In Güney Dal's *Europastraße 5*, published in 1981, the father of a Turkish guest worker dies while living illegally in Berlin with his son and daughter-in-law. The distraught couple needs to find a way to dispose of the corpse, because its discovery could result in their deportation. They squeeze the dead body into a packing carton, tie it onto the luggage rack on top of their car, and set off for Turkey. Despite the fact that their car is stopped at border crossings, that a strange stench emanates from the carton, and that it actually falls off the rack several times, the corpse is not discovered. The couple is arrested only once they are in Turkey, because the police find an illegal printing press in the car. In the end, the unwitting son is charged with his father's murder as they suspect him of an anarchist conspiracy against the Turkish state. The major difference between Dal's text and Zaimoglu's "Die Beerdigungs-Story" is that in the former the corpse is not allowed to remain in Germany, whereas in the latter it is buried there with due observation of Islamic law. In both texts, however, presumption of criminality plays an important role. The difference is that in *Europastraße 5*, the real victim is the son while in "Die Beerdigungs-Story" the social prejudice of alleged criminality has no consequence other than making the narrator nauseous.

In "Minor Chords? Migration, Murder, and Multiculturalism," Leslie A. Adelson reads Güney Dal's novel as a story of disorientation. The function of the father in the text, about whose life the reader learns through flashbacks, is that of a representative of a particular historical time which he attempts to keep alive by telling stories. With his death, this particular narrative discourse becomes obsolete as well. His son Salim, a fisherman in Turkey before he became a guest worker in Germany, has no use for his father's historical knowledge as it "becomes displaced by a changed historical configuration for which Salim himself can find no adequate narrative."[32] "With the change in livelihood and locale ... Salim loses his personal and narrative moorings," as Adelson concludes.[33] She calls *Europastraße 5* "a sophisticated account of an epochal sense of disorientation," a disorientation that is presented "as a historical and epistemological caesura of national, international, and transnational dimensions."[34] A comparison of Dal's and Zaimoglu's texts sheds light on the different positions of first and second-generation Turkish writers in Germany. While disorientation is a central trope in migrant writing of the early 1980s – in *Abschied der zerschellten Jahre* Franco Biondi illustrates how Costas's ethnic memory cannot save Mamo from his fatal disorientation – migrant writing of the 1990s has moved to a stage of self-affirmation.

Feridun Zaimoglu proves that the *Kanaksta* is able to speak for himself and on his own terms. Like Zehra Çirak and Akif Pirinçci, Zaimoglu contributes to dismantling traditional notions of what constitutes "German literature" through abrogation and appropriation. Yet, unlike Zehra Çirak and Renan Demirkan, he does not believe in the reconciling power of hybrid identity, which, in his opinion, is a myth invented by social workers. With the grotesque realism and exclusionary politics displayed in his writing, Zaimoglu and his *Kanakstas* have become the German reader's worst nightmare.

Conclusion

As I am interested in paradigms of counterdiscursive strategies, I have chosen to analyse a limited number of texts rather than offer a comprehensive survey, and just as the counterdiscursive is not a universal feature of postcolonial writing, I do not suggest that it is a universal feature of "marginal" writing in Germany. Indeed, Stephen Slemon draws attention to the pitfalls of assuming that Third and Fourth-World[1] writing is necessarily oppositional and always resorts to counter discourse. According to Slemon, this assumption dismisses "realist" writing emerging from these cultural locations, as well as it "overlook[s] the range of anti-colonialist gestures which inhabit First-World, or imperial, writing itself."[2] Without privileging a specific discourse, I nevertheless demonstrate in this study that in the 1980s and 1990s writers from various cultural backgrounds engaged in oppositional aesthetics in order to construct their own version of "Germany" and to write back to the German canon.

Interestingly enough, mainstream German literature of the 1980s has also been described as oppositional. In the 1980s this literature shifted away from the new subjectivism of the 1970s, placing renewed emphasis on form. In their "counter [hi]stories" "Gegengeschichten"[3] writers such as Herbert Achternbusch, Ludwig Fels, Bodo Kirchhoff, Alexander Kluge, and Botho Strauss not only reconceptualize the relationship between text and reality, but also demonstrate a loss of faith in the construction of meaning. While the oppositional gesture in these "Gegengeschichten" lies in their authors' heightened awareness of the restorative potential of aesthetics, the restorative potential of the counter discourse in which "marginal" writers engage is quite different. The oppositional impulse in the texts that I have discussed, whether manifested in "countercanonical" discourse, postcolonial picaresque, hybridity, rewriting of genre, or grotesque realism, is prompted by the exclusionary politics of the dominant culture. The oppositional strategies used in the rewriting of Germany from the margins expose the assumptions that underlie German public discourses and dismantle them, that is, destabilize notions of Germanness, Jewishness, Turkishness, and so on.

Mainstream publishers, readers, and critics, however, still seek a voyeuristic look into the allegedly exotic world of "marginal" writers. As much as these writers attempt to come to terms with their identity, they are defined by their publishers as Jewish/migrant/East German, not simply as German writers. Emphasizing the Jewish/migrant/East German identity of an author, whether that author accepts this designation or not, does have an effect on the reception and the sales of the books. Such exoticization goes hand in hand with homogenization. As Henry Louis Gates observes, "the threat to the margin comes not from assimilation or dissolution – from any attempt to denude it of its defiant alterity – but, on the contrary, from the center's attempts to preserve that alterity, which result in the homogenization of the other as, simply, other."[4]

As I have shown, however, there is no unified body of contemporary Jewish/migrant/East German writing in Germany today, and the writers' ethnic background, their gender, age, and generation affect in any case the conceptualization of the text. Nor do German Jewish, migrant, or "East German" writers speak in one voice. Yet their voices were not clearly heard prior to the 1980s. Not until the mid-1980s did contemporary German Jewish writers begin to write about their lives in present-day Germany. Furthermore, discussions evoked by the provocative work of Henryk Broder, Dan Diner, Esther Dischereit, Richard Chaim Schneider, and Rafael Seligmann, among others, demonstrate the influence of these writers on contemporary German culture. The political events that took place in the 1980s formed the backdrop against which a new self-awareness of second-generation Jews emerged, as Richard Chaim Schneider demonstrates in *Zwischenwelten*. This writing deals not only with the question of Jewish identity *per se*, but also with the vicissitudes of Jewish male and female identities and with intergenerational conflicts.

Migrant literature underwent a paradigm shift in the 1980s as well. While in the 1970s migrant writing appeared in anthologies edited by German scholars and published by mainstream publishers, in the 1980s and 1990s migrant writers started opening their own publishing houses, developing their own cultural theories, and organizing their own conferences. Furthermore, beginning with Akif Pirinçci's *Tränen sind immer das Ende*, published in 1980, most migrant literature has been shifting away from the discourse of "Betroffenheit" and social realism and has become more self-reflexive, hybrid, intertextual, and counterdiscursive.

Self-reflexiveness, intertextuality, and oppositional practice also characterize the prose of those writers born in the GDR who launched their literary careers after the fall of the Wall. As I have demonstrated, both Thomas Brussig and Kerstin Jentzsch use intertextuality, satire, and irony to deconstruct the mythological qualities that the unification process had assumed. Now that the fall of the wall and the unification have lost their immediate fascination for writers, it will be interesting to see if and how the texts of young writers born in the GDR will change, and if in five or ten years from now their readers will still think of them as GDR writers. In his polemic article "Die Wiedervereinigung der deutschen Literatur" ["The Reunification of German Literature"], Jurek Becker predicted that to become part of "West German" literature, "East German" literature has to become less serious and more entertaining because nothing bores "West" German readers more than social criticism. And what more efficient way of standing up to the entertainment industry, Becker asks, than by becoming a part of it?

As the kind of oppositional practice in German literature that I discuss in this book is very much a phenomenon of the 1980s and 1990s, it remains to be seen how margin and centre will construct themselves in the new millennium. Will the changes to the citizenship law that went into effect in January 2000 also change the notions of exclusivity that most Germans still entertain with regard to what it means to be "German"? If receiving German citizenship will allow migrants a stronger feeling of belonging, will migrant writing consequently become less oppositional and counterdiscursive? How many generations will it take for Germans to stop thinking of themselves as East Germans and West Germans? If Jurek Becker was right in his 1990 prediction, will it soon be impossible to distinguish between the "two German literatures" because both will only be concerned with sales figures? Will the relationship between German Jews and Germans continue to be defined as "negative symbiosis," a relationship that puts Jews in a position where they have to react, as Richard Chaim Schneider puts it? Ultimately, will contemporary German Jewish literature be perceived as an integral part of German literature?

Considering all these issues, it is important not to forget that the "margin" plays an important part in defining its relationship with the centre. Therefore the "margin's" complicity in existing power structures needs to be taken into account. As Stephen Slemon points out, "resistance itself is ... never *purely* resistance, never *simply* there in the text or the interpretive community, but is always *necessarily* complicit in the apparatus it seeks to transgress."[5] The fact that the writers discussed in this book write for the German reader implicates them in the creation of certain reader expectations. Some of the writers, like Esther Dischereit, whom I quote in the Introduction, are more disturbed by their dependence on the German reader than others. For writers like Lea Fleischmann and Barbara Honigmann, who choose not to live in Germany, the relationship to their German-speaking audience is even more precarious. Assimilation is an additional force to contend with for those who were born some place else and now live in Germany. The rhetorical question that Zehra Çirak's lyric speaker asks herself, "how can I resist becoming one of the well-fed and jaded and westernized?" reflects the writer's own dilemma. Such ambivalence of textual resistance is caused by the fact that it is situated between systems and between discourses, as Jenny Sharpe notes.[6]

Last but not least, as I have stated in the Preface, the fact that German literature and culture are being rewritten from the margins has ramifications for North American German Studies. Critics like Karen Jankowsky, Jeffrey Peck, Azade Seyhan, and Arlene Teraoka draw attention to the "belatedness" of the discipline, that is, its resistance to theory, revision of the canon, and curriculum reform.

Lutz P. Koepnick takes his criticism a step further by sounding the following note of warning: "For instead of going cross-eyed from curiously jealous gazes at the institutional situation of *Germanistik* in Germany, American[7] German Studies will remain a viable force only if it learns how to exploit its own double dislocation as its very source of insight, inspiration, and self-reflection."[8] "Marginal" texts need to be integrated into, not simply added onto, German department reading lists and course syllabi. Their oppositional potential lends itself to an interactive and dynamic constellation of texts and invites a more conflict-oriented approach to literature. As today's Germany is very much a society in transition, a society that has come to terms neither with the Holocaust nor with unification, whose demography, economy, and social system have been undergoing massive changes, and which has just reformed its citizenship laws, its literary voices will become more and more heterogeneous. Centre and margin will therefore continue to reconstitute and redefine themselves.

Notes

INTRODUCTION

1 Lutz Hoffmann, *Die unvollendete Republik: Zwischen Einwanderungsland und deutschem Nationalstaat*, 23–5.

2 However, one needs to keep in mind that Germany's foreign population today is composed not only of the guest workers and their children and grandchildren but also of asylum seekers – currently the Federal Republic accepts approximately 90,000 per year – and repatriated Germans from East European countries. The influx of these "Aussiedler" increased immensely in the late 1980s because the political climate east of the Iron Curtain had changed. For a critical overview of German integration policy in the twentieth century see Cem Özdemir, *Currywurst und Döner: Integration in Deutschland.*

3 Klaus J. Bade, "Einwanderung und Gesellschaftspolitik in Deutschland – quo vadis Bundesrepublik?" 250.

4 (German) Jewish fears of renewed nationalism and anti-Jewish sentiments in Germany are discussed, for example, by Sander L. Gilman in "German Reunification and the Jews," Cilly Kugelmann in "Tell Them in America We're Still Alive!: The Jewish Community in the Federal Republic," and Frank Stern "The 'Jewish Question'; in the 'German Question,' 1945–1990: Reflections in Light of November 9th, 1989."

5 See, for example, Zafer Şenocak's comments in his collection of essays *Atlas des tropischen Deutschland* [*Atlas of Tropical Germany*]. Leslie A. Adelson is currently preparing an English translation of this text.

6 According to Arlene A. Teraoka, "there were twenty-three hundred documented crimes of violence against foreigners in 1991, ten times the number of incidents in 1990." *East, West, and Others,* 201.

7 See Uli Linke, "Murderous Fantasies: Violence, Memory, and Selfhood in Germany."

8 Roland Kirbach, among others, comments on the increased "self-ethnicization" of the Turks in Germany in *Die Zeit,* 23 May 1997. He claims that the Turks in Germany "have become more Turkish" as a reaction to a decrease in both Turkish and German willingness to communicate with each other. While a few years ago, young Turks, for example, would have been bashful about being seen in public with their headscarf-wearing mothers, today according to Kirbach, they are proud of these symbols of ethnic belonging and solidarity.

9 Franco Biondi, who arrived in Germany at the age of eighteen, is the only exception. According to Inter Nationes, in 1996 approximately seven million foreigners [8.5 percent of Germany's total population] lived in Germany. More than half of these seven million have been living there for more than ten years. Numbering more than two million, Turks constituted by far the largest group of non-German residents. See Irmgard Ackermann, *Fremde Augen-Blicke: Multikulturelle Literatur in Deutschland,* 7.

10 Y. Michal Bodemann estimates the total Jewish population in Germany at the time the article was written at anywhere between 50,000 and 70,000. According to Bodemann, the vast majority of present-day Jewry in Germany is of East European descent, "with only a small fraction of descendants of prewar German Jewish stock living there today." "A Reemergence of German Jewry?" 55. See also Igor Reichlin's article "Making a Living – Jews in German Economic Life."

11 As Abdul R. JanMohamed points out, "works of minority writers are linked by the imperative to negate, in various ways, the prior negation of his [*sic*] culture by the dominators. Even though such an imperative may be initially entirely negative, it implies an affirmative search for an alternative that is yet unarticulated." "Humanism and Minority Literature: Toward a Definition of Counter-hegemonic Discourse," 296.

12 Arlene Teraoka, "*Gastarbeiterliteratur*," 297.

13 The term "counterdiscourse" was coined by Richard Terdiman to refer to the practice of symbolic resistance in his study of nineteenth-century French literature. The term has been adopted by postcolonial critics to describe the complex ways in which a dominant discourse might be challenged from the margins.

14 Helen Tiffin, "Post-Colonial Literatures and Counter-Discourse."

15 Other critical works, besides those already mentioned, that focus on oppositional practice in literature and are useful in the discussion of minority literatures are Ross Chambers' *Room for Maneuver: Reading (the) Oppositional in Narrative*, Arun Mukherjee's *Readings from a Hyphenated Space: Oppositional Aesthetics*, and Doris Sommer's "Resistant Texts and Incompetent Readers." Critics also often apply Julia Kristeva's notions of the semiotic as a subversive and disruptive force in discussing the counterdiscursive function in minority discourses. And last but not least, Gilles Deleuze's and Félix Guattari's discussion of "minor literature" in *Kafka: Toward a Minor Literature* is frequently evoked in critical readings of minority writing. These two critics refer to literature as "minor" when it is forced into a position of otherness on account of its nonterritorial status. They claim that "minority literature" is characterized by three features: "A high coefficient of deterritorialization" in its language, the fact that "everything in [it] is political," and "that in it everything takes on a collective value" (*Kafka: Toward a Minor Literature*, 16–17). If one writes from the margins, Deleuze and Guattari claim, "this situation allows the writer all the more the possibility to express another possible community and to forge the means for another consciousness and another sensibility" (17).

16 Russell Ferguson, "Introduction: Invisible Center," 9.

17 I am using the word migrant here and in the following for lack of a better term to refer to ethnic-minority writing. I opt for this term as Sneja Gunew and other Australian critics have used it in focusing on the subversive potential of the writing to which they apply it. The German equivalent *Migrantenliteratur*, on the other hand, has more negative than positive connotations, and most second-generation writers are critical of the term.

18 See Annette Wierschke's *Schreiben als Selbstbehauptung: Kulturkonflikt und Identität in den Werken von Aysel Özakin, Alev Tekinay and Emine Sevgi Özdamar* as well as Karen Jankowsky's "'German'

Literature Contested: The 1991 Ingeborg-Bachmann-Prize Debate, 'Cultural Diversity,' and Emine Sevgi Özdamar."

19 Jusuf Naoum, "Aus dem Getto heraus," 79.

20 "Ich möchte gegen die Fremde in der Sprache anschreiben." Franco Biondi, "Die Fremde wohnt in der Sprache," 32. All translations from German to English in this book, including those of titles, are mine unless indicated otherwise. Translating texts that play with and undermine the language in which they are written is always a challenge, and certain inadequacies are unfortunately inevitable.

21 "Wir schreiben immer, fast absichtslos, gegen die herrschenden literarischen Regeln und Normen der deutschen Literatur." Suleman Taufiq, "Natürlich: Kritik," 77.

22 Rüdiger Krechel quotes Maria Frisé, who, in a review in the *Frankfurter Allgemeine,* criticizes Biondi for using ungrammatical German: "Unfortunately, the pages are covered with false images, incorrect subjunctives, and stylistic howlers" ["Aber leider wimmeln die Seiten von falschen Bildern, falschen Konjunktiven, lächerlichen Stilblüten"]. In *Werkheft Literatur: Franco Biondi,* 54.

23 Jusuf Naoum, "Aus dem Getto heraus, 79.

24 "So reden die Gastarbeiter nicht." Jusuf Naoum, "Aus dem Getto heraus," 80.

25 "Ikonen des Fremden – sie sind die perfekten anderen." Quoted in Adelson, "Opposing Oppositions," 305.

26 David Horrocks and Eva Kolinsky, eds. *Turkish Culture in German Society Today,* Introduction, xx.

27 Leslie Adelson, "Migrants' Literature or German Literature?" 383.

28 See Annette Wierschke, 66.

29 Werner Sollors calls for a move "beyond ethnicity" in the discussion of "ethnic" literatures. He criticizes literary critics of "ethnic" literature for putting too much emphasis on "ethnic" difference: "Instead of understanding their texts as codes for a socialization into ethnic groups and into America, readers have overemphasized and exaggerated the (frequently exoticized) ethnic particularity of the works ... The literature is often read and evaluated against an elusive concept of authenticity, and the question of who is entitled to interpret the literature is given undue emphasis." *Beyond Ethnicity: Consent and Descent in American Culture,* 11.

30 "Talking back" is an expression that bell hooks uses to identify the ability to "speak as an equal to an authority figure" that allows women/women of colour to move from an object to a subject position. *Talking Back: Thinking Feminist, Thinking Black,* 5.

31 Compare also Françoise Lionnet's discussion of *métissage* in *Autobiographical Voices: Race, Gender, Self-Portraiture*.

32 According to Zaimoglu, the term *Kanaksta* is formed by fusing *Kanake* and *Gangster*. The term *Kanake* was used during Germany's colonial rule to refer in a demeaning manner to the local people. In contemporary German it is a derogatory term for a person from a visible minority. Zaimoglu uses the term subversively, so that it becomes empowering.

33 The three texts that have provoked the greatest number of postcolonial rewritings are Shakespeare's *The Tempest*, Daniel Defoe's *Robinson Crusoe*, and Joseph Conrad's *Heart of Darkness*. Writers such as Samuel Selvon in *Moses Ascending* and J.M. Coetzee in *Foe* write back to *Robinson Crusoe*; Wilson Harris in *Heartland*, James Ngugi in *The River Between*, and Timothy Findley in *Headhunter* rewrite *Heart of Darkness*; and Audrey Thomas in *Munchmeyer and Prospero on the Island* and Randolph Stow in *Visitants* rewrite *The Tempest* [compare Diana Brydon, *Decolonising Fictions*]. All these writers re-imagine the texts of their precursors and write them into their own time and into their own frame of reference by glossing, subverting, and transforming them.

34 For a discussion of how discursive practices help to generate social reality see Uli Linke, "Murderous Fantasies: Violence, Memory, and Selfhood in Germany" and Michelle Mattson, "Refugees in Germany: Invasion or Invention?"

35 Nora Räthzel, "Germany: one race, one nation?" 46.

36 Räthzel, 46.

37 Räthzel, 46–7.

38 Andreas Huyssen, "After the Wall: The Failure of German Intellectuals," 125.

39 Huyssen, 125.

40 Huyssen, 125.

41 Sander Gilman made this comment in a lecture entitled "Daniel Goldhagen and Young German-Jewish Writers" at the University of British Columbia on 17 September 1997.

42 Elena Lappin, ed. *Jewish Voices – German Words: Growing Up Jewish in Postwar Germany and Austria*, 10.

43 Jack Zipes, "The Contemporary German Fascination for Things Jewish: Toward a Jewish Minor Culture," 16. See also Jeannie Marshall, "Suddenly in Germany, it's Cool to be Jewish."

44 However, Zipes is quick to point out that, by expressing this hope, he does not "want to minimize the present danger of the radical

right in Germany that threatens Jewish culture or the fear
expressed by many Jews living in Germany, who may eventually
emigrate," 16–17.

45 Jack Zipes, 19.

46 As Ruth-Ellen Boetcher Joeres and Elizabeth Mittman claim: The
essay is "a site for critical reflection, for subversive ... thought" and
"it is generally consigned to a netherworld of something different,
borderland." *The Politics of the Essay: Feminist Perspectives*, 12.

47 See Barbara Foley, "Fact, Fiction, Fascism: Testimony and Mimesis
in Holocaust Narratives."

48 I provide a detailed discussion of the Fassbinder affair in chapter 5.

49 In 1984, when the leaders of the western powers met to celebrate
the anniversary of the World War II landings in Normandy, Chancellor Helmut Kohl was understandably not invited. After having
met with François Mitterand at a military cemetery in Verdun, Kohl
invited Ronald Reagan to visit the cemetery in Bitburg in May 1985
to pay joint homage to the war dead and as a final act of reconcilia-
tion between the former enemies. When Jewish organizations pro-
tested because there are graves of members of the *Wehrmacht* and
the SS in this cemetery, Reagan announced that he had also sched-
uled a visit to Bergen-Belsen. Protests were then voiced not only
within the Jewish community but also in the US Senate and House
of Representatives.

50 The German historians' debate erupted in the summer of 1986 in
reaction to historian Ernst Nolte's article "Vergangenheit, die nicht
vergehen will" ["The Past That Will Not Go Away"], published in
the *Frankfurter Allgemeine*. It evolved into a major intellectual
conflict over the implications of Germany's Nazi past for contemporary West German identity. Ernst Nolte, one of Germany's most
controversial right-wing historians, argued, among other things,
that the Holocaust was not unique but can be compared to the
atrocities committed in the Soviet Union under Stalin.

51 See Jack Zipes, "The Contemporary Fascination for Things Jewish"
as well as Helmut Peitsch, "Autobiographical Writing as *Vergangenheitsbewältigung* (Mastering the Past)."

52 The word "Holocaust" entered the German language in the wake
of this film. There is no German word for the annihilation of the
Jews. To escape the "commercialization" evoked by the term "Holocaust," Jews now tend to avoid the word and use the Hebrew word
"Shoah" instead.

53 Anton Kaes, "1979 The American television series *Holocaust* is shown in West Germany," 784.
54 According to Thomas Nolden, approximately 2000 Jews lived in the GDR in 1989. *Junge jüdische Literatur*, 21.
55 A passage of this novel has been included in Elena Lappin's anthology *Jewish Voices, German Words: Growing Up Jewish in Postwar Germany and Austria*. Krishna Winston, who translated the texts into English, opted for this translation of the title of Honigmann's novel. The original title, however, is ambiguous and could be translated as *Novel about a Child* or *Novel by a Child*.
56 Nineteenth-century anti-Semitic discourse about the Jews denied them a proper place in Western European culture because of their supposed orientalism. Jewish orientalism manifested itself, according to anti-Semitic beliefs, in the Jews' nomadism and desert instincts.
57 Elena Lappin, 9.
58 Quoted in Sander Gilman, *Jews in Today's German Culture*, 60.
59 Barbara Frischmuth's novel was published in English translation by Ariadne in 1998.
60 Russell Ferguson, 13.

CHAPTER ONE

1 Diana Brydon and Helen Tiffin, *Decolonising Fictions*, 77.
2 Helen Tiffin, "Post-Colonial Literatures and Counter-Discourse," 23.
3 *Decolonising Fictions*, 78.
4 Harald Weinrich, "Um eine deutsche Literatur von außen bittend," 913.
5 Weinrich, 920.
6 Franco Biondi left Italy at the age of eighteen to work as a welder in Germany. He published his first poetry in 1979.
7 Heidrun Suhr, "Ausländerliteratur: Minority Literature in the Federal Republic of Germany," 91–2.
8 Suhr, 92.
9 Marilya Veteto-Conrad, *Finding a Voice: Identity and the Works of German-Language Turkish Writers in the Federal Republic of Germany to 1990*, 80–81.
10 See Introduction, 6.
11 "Eine sich ereignete unerhörte Begebenheit." Konrad Höfer, ed. *Johann Peter Eckermann: Gespräche mit Goethe*, 204
12 A.D. Harvey, "Why the 'Novelle'?" 165.

13 Harvey, 166.

14 Paul Heyse claimed that a *Novelle*, to be effective, needs a central leitmotif, which he called the *Falke* [falcon] after Boccaccio's ninth story of the fifth day in *Il Decamerone*.

15 Compare *Deutsches Ausländerrecht* [*German Foreigners Law*], 1. *Ausländergesetz*, paragraphs 17 and 29.

16 The *Studienkolleg* prepares international students for university in Germany. The language of instruction is German.

17 See Robert C. Holub, "Realism, Repetition, Repression: The Nature of Desire in *Romeo und Julia auf dem Dorfe*, 475.

18 Interestingly enough, Biondi's parents were showpeople who travelled the country, performing at markets and fairs.

19 In this context, it is important to remember that on 17 June 1981, fifteen renowned German professors from various faculties signed the "Heidelberger Manifest" in which they voiced their concern about the influx of "foreigners" into Germany. The manifesto promotes foreign aid to make it both unnecessary for guest workers to look for work elsewhere and to reclaim living space for the Germans, *Die Zeit*, 5 February 1982.

20 "Ansonsten bin ich aus dem Niemandsland ... genauso wie der Odysseus vor dem Zyklopen; bekanntlich hat er vor dem Zyklopen Niemand geheißen, um seine Haut zu retten. Genau dasselbe geschieht auch mit mir." *Abschied der zerschellten Jahre*, 83.

21 The overgrown acre serves as a playground for Sali and Vrenchen where they play free of moral restraints and unchecked by society. Their cruel play with the naked doll, its dismemberment, and the children's burial of the doll's head, in which they trapped a fly, foreshadows the events of the lovers' last day. Furthermore, just as the field stands for nature as opposed to culture, Vrenchen is associated with nature and described as "wild" and unconventional.

22 Mamo's shooting of the representative of a state that is depicted as corrupted by fascist undercurrents invites comparison with Mario's [the similarity of the protagonists' names may be taken as indication that the analogy is intentional] shooting of Cipolla in Thomas Mann's "Mario und der Zauberer" ["Mario and the magician"]. In neither of the two texts does the murder signal a liberating end for the protagonist.

23 "Ein süßer Mandelkern ist meine Lieb zu Dir!" and "Wenn Du dies Herz gegessen, vergiß dies Sprüchlein nicht: Viel eh'r als meine Liebe mein braunes Auge bricht!." *Romeo und Julia auf dem Dorfe*, 115.

24 "Sie halten den Spieß in der Hand."

25 "Die wissen schon alles im voraus. Es gibt überhaupt keine Wahrheit heutzutage. Immer wird der Spieß umgedreht." *Abschied der zerschellten Jahre*, 124.

26 Hans Wysling, "Und immer wieder kehrt Odysseus heim: Das 'Fabelhafte' bei Gottfried Keller," 155.

27 Wysling, 154.

28 "Tatsächlich ist meine Wohnung eine Vorstufe des Himmels geworden. " *Abschied der zerschellten Jahre*, 141.

29 Elizabeth A. Flynn, "Gender and Reading," 268.

30 Flynn, 268.

31 Flynn, 271.

32 Although Akif was not born in Germany, the novel makes it clear that German is the only language in which he communicates, and that he feels at home in "western" literature and culture.

33 During the early phase of labour recruitment, the majority of guest workers were men.

34 *Literatur der Betroffenheit* loosely translates as "literature of affliction" or "literature of the affected." Jusuf Naoum and Suleman Taufiq also contributed to this essay.

35 "Selbsthilfe zur Verteidigung der Identität." Franco Biondi and Rafik Schami, "Literatur der Betroffenheit," 133.

36 In the GDR, the clash between the generation who had built the state in defiance of "western" values, and their children, who had never lived under any other system but were drawn to western popular culture and fashion, was particularly strong in the 1970s.

37 "War das das Ende? Dumme, schwere, vernichtende Arbeit? Gleichzeitig wußte ich, daß es auch mit Christa nicht mehr so weitergehen würde … Sie eines Tages Richterin oder Anwältin und ich ein bekloppter Holzkopf von einem Bühnenarbeiter." *Tränen sind immer das Ende*, 149.

38 "Hiermit wurde ich also ein richtiger Arbeiter, was mein Vater mir seit meiner Kindheit prophezeit hatte und wovor er mich mit allen Mitteln zu schützen versucht hatte." *Tränen sind immer das Ende*, 93.

39 "Sohn, das ist keine Arbeit für dich. Nicht für einen jungen Menschen. Die Oper macht dich kaputt, das hältst du nicht aus. Schau mich an, Sohn! Ich arbeite seit siebzehn Jahren hier. So sieht ein Mann aus, der seit siebzehn Jahren hier arbeitet." *Tränen sind immer das Ende*, 120–1.

40 "Der Kasten hieß ... 'Treff' und war überfüllt wie Dachau." *Tränen sind immer das Ende,* 5.

41 "[Sie] haben ihn mit diesem 'Eumel' gehänselt bis zum Vergasen." *Tränen sind immer das Ende,* 39. "Bis zum Vergasen" cannot be translated literally into English. The expression refers to the gassing of victims in the concentration camps and is still occasionally used in contemporary German, the younger generation often being unaware of the origin of the phrase.

42 See Introduction, note 15.

CHAPTER TWO

1 Kerstin Jentzsch was born in 1964 and Thomas Brussig in 1965. *Wende* [turn, transition] is a term used to refer to the fall of the Wall and its aftermath.

2 See, for example, the plethora of "ethnic" American picaresque novels written during the early decades of the twentieth century such as Nathaniel West's *The Dream Life of Balso Snell,* Saul Bellow's *The Adventures of Augie March* , and Ralph Ellison's *Invisible Man,* as well as more recent novels, such as Gish Jen's *Typical American,* Natalie Goldberg's *Banana Rose,* Lois-Ann Yamanaka's *Wild Meat and the Bully Burgers,* and Bharati Mukherjee's *Leave It to Me,* to name but a few.

3 Dan Diner in "Negative Symbiose: Deutsche und Juden nach Auschwitz" ["Negative Symbiosis: Germans and Jews after Auschwitz"] refers to today's relationship of Germans and Jews as "negative symbiosis," a "communality of opposites," as this relationship is defined by their roles in the Holocaust as perpetrators and victims respectively. The English translation of Diner's essay, "Negative Symbiosis: Germans and Jews after Auschwitz," was published in *Reworking the Past: Hitler, the Holocaust, and the Historians' Debate,* ed. Peter Baldwin. Boston: Beacon Press Books 1990.

4 For a discussion of censorship under GDR socialism see, for example, Andrea Jäger, "Schriftsteller-Identität und Zensur: Über die Bedingungen des Schreibens im 'realen Sozialismus.'"

5 William Walker, "Satire and Societal Criticism in the GDR Picaresque Novel," 161.

6 Walker, 161.

7 The Eighth Party Congress of the Socialist Unity Party (SED), held in 1971, at which Erich Honecker gave GDR artists license to deviate

within limits from the strict rules of social realism, marked a turning point for GDR literature that made possible the publication of
novels such as Ulrich Plenzdorf's *Die neuen Leiden des jungen W.*

8 See my discussion of Ulrich Plenzdorf's *Die neuen Leiden des jungen
   W.* as a rewriting of the "Ankunftsroman" in chapter 1.

9 See, for example, Peter Bender, "Vereinigen können sich nur
   Gleiche: Über die dreifache Enteignung der Ostdeutschen." Bender
   argues that the GDR has been "expropriated threefold": economi-
   cally, politically, and morally.

10 "Wenn man aber Kolonialisierung nicht mit dem Einmarsch von
   Kolonialtruppen … gleichsetzt, sondern das Entscheidende ins
   Auge faßt: die Zerstörung einer 'einheimischen' Wirtschafts-
   struktur, die Ausbeutung der vorhandenen ökonomischen Res-
   sourcen, die soziale Liquidation nicht nur der politischen Elite,
   sondern auch der Intelligenz eines Landes sowie die Zerstörung
   der gewachsenen – wie auch immer problematischen – Identität
   einer Bevölkerung, so hat sich in der Tat in der ehemaligen DDR im
   präzisen Sinne des Begriffs ein Kolonialisierungsprozeß vollzo-
   gen." Wolfgang Dümcke and Fritz Vilmar, eds. *Kolonialisierung der
   DDR: Kritische Analysen und Alternativen des Einigungsprozesses*, 13.

11 Bernd Hüppauf concludes with the words: "Sie [die kleinen
   Freiheiten] zu erkennen, setzt jedoch voraus, sich von der Angst
   vor dem Tod der Literatur in den grenzenlosen Weiten der
   Moderne zu befreien und die Sprache aus der Welt der
   schützenden Mauern herauszuführen." ["To be able to recognize
   the small liberties one needs to free oneself from the fear of the
   dissolution of literature in the borderless realms of modernity and
   to liberate language from protective walls."] "Moral oder Sprache:
   DDR-Literatur vor der Moderne," 230.

12 See Dennis Tate, "Trapped in the Past? The Identity Problems of
   East German Writers since the *Wende*," 13.

13 "Was bin ich? DDRler oder Deutscher? Osteuropäer – anhand der
   politischen Sozialisation definiert? Mitteleuropäer, was die Mental-
   ität betrifft? Durch ein Buch erklärte ich mich zum Berliner. Ostber-
   liner oder Berliner generell? Oder prägt die Thüringer Herkunft
   doch stärker, als ich es lange wahrhaben wollte? … Als deutsch-
   sprachiger Schriftsteller fühle ich mich auf jeden Fall, dem
   schweizerischen und österreichischen Autoren verwandter als den
   bundesdeutschen. Doch auch der polnischen und tschechischen
   Literatur fühle ich mich in ihrer oft respektlos kritischen Haltung

mehr verbunden als jener der DDR. Was also bin ich?" Lutz Rathenow, "Nachdenken über Deutschland," 285.

14 Roger Woods, "'Nuancen und Zwischentöne' versus 'muskelprotzende Prosa': Autobiography and the Project of Explaining 'How it Was' in the GDR," 43.

15 Nancy A. Lauckner, "The Treatment of Problems of Integration in Some Recent Works by Authors from the Former GDR," 223.

16 See Wolfgang Emmerich, "Status melancholicus: Zur Transformation der Utopie in der DDR-Literatur."

17 In 1996, Jentzsch published a sequel to this novel entitled *Ankunft der Pandora* [*Pandora's Arrival*], a title which ironically alludes to the "Ankunftsroman."

18 Most of the hostile feelings in "West" German criticism aimed at Wolf's narrative were aroused by its publication date. *Was bleibt* was written in 1979 [according to the narrator and/or author] and reworked in 1989, and if it had appeared in 1979 rather than after the fall of the Wall, it would most likely have been hailed as an attack on a totalitarian regime. Many critics who vilified the book also make the mistake of taking the narrator for the author herself.

19 Dysfunctional families appear in a great number of GDR novels, and the absence of fathers is particularly noticeable.

20 For example, Lisa is reprimanded by her headmaster for giving an eight-year-old girl permission to stay inside, while she takes the rest of the class on an excursion. Thereby she complies with the wishes of the parents, who do not want their daughter to be exposed to radioactive fallout from Chernobyl.

21 The giant penis as a "liberating tool" is a motif also used in Gerhard Zwerenz' picaresque novel *Casanova oder der Kleine Herr in Krieg und Frieden* [*Casanova or the Little Guy in War and Peace* (1966).

22 "Was können wir Ihnen versprechen? Kein leichtes, aber ein nützliches und interessantes Leben. Keinen schnellen Wohlstand, aber Mitwirkung an großen Veränderungen. Christa Wolf, *Im Dialog*, 169.

23 Peter C. Pfeiffer, "The National Identity of the GDR: Antifascism, Historiography, Literature," 25.

24 Hermann Glaser, and with him many other critics, however, see the peaceful revolution as a "result of many individual acts which went above and beyond what people in the West envision as civic courage." "The Future Requires an Origin: East-West German Identity, the Opportunities and Difficulties of Cultural Politics," 77.

25 "Missing link [English in the original] der jüngsten deutschen Geschichte." *Helden wie wir*, 323.
26 John Borneman, "Time-Space Compression and the Continental Divide in German Subjectivity," 114.
27 Christa Wolf, *Voraussetzungen einer Erzählung*, 53.
28 "The good development of socialism" and "harmony of continuity and renewal."
29 Derek Lewis, "The Role of Language in the Fall of the GDR and the Aftermath," 125.
30 See Peter Zima, "Der Mythos der Monosemie."
31 "Wachstum, Wohlstand, Stabilität."
32 "Du sitzt an Deinem griechischen Strand und denkst nach über die Ursprünge der Menschheit, der Demokratie und der menschlichen Seele. In manchen Augenblicken spürst Du Deine Befindlichkeit, Deine Ohnmacht, Deine Hilflosigkeit." *Seit die Götter ratlos sind*, 415.
33 As Christiane Zehl Romero points out, the young woman in Wolf's text, representative of a more independent and daring generation, is modelled after the writer Gabriele Stötzer-Kachold, born in 1953. The writer was imprisoned following her protests against Wolf Biermann's expatriation in 1976. See "Sexual Politics and Christa Wolf's *Was bleibt.*"
34 "Jeder Satz sei wahr … Diese paar Seiten könnten sie wieder ins Gefängnis bringen." *Was bleibt*, 76.
35 Tiffin, 22.

CHAPTER THREE

1 "Schweifen und Abschweifen." Chaim Noll, "Enge oder ein Versuch, Amerikanern Deutschland zu erklären," 91. This essay is included in Noll's collection of essays *Leben ohne Deutschland*.
2 Ania Walwicz. *Writing*, 34.
3 Walwicz, 67.
4 Sneja Gunew, "Beyond the echo," 63.
5 Quoted in Gunew, "Denaturalizing," 105.
6 Zehra Çirak, *Vogel auf dem Rücken eines Elefanten* [*Bird on the Back of an Elephant*].
7 In July 1996 political representatives of the German-speaking countries signed the proposal for a German spelling reform in Vienna. Since 1 August 1998, the revised spelling has been taught in all

German [with the exception of those in Schleswig-Holstein], Austrian, and Swiss schools.

8 The final stanza of this poem, which contains the quoted line, reads as follows: dann lese ich die Punkte auf / und rufe das Zeichen aus / falsch getippt / bin ich in allen Zweifelsfällen / und Vorschriften die nachkommen / die stechenden Stichwörter / die schlechten Träume / der Silben und der Trennungen / und sind wir uns nur sachverwandt / damals wie heute hat man den Traum / der Aufgabe die Rechtschreibung / im gesamten Raum / einheitlich zu riegeln.

9 Oliver, *Weil ich dieses Land liebe* [*Because I Love This Land*]. Depending on context, *einfallen* means "to collapse," "to invade," "to occur to," or "to enter from above." *Auffallen* can mean "to attract attention," "to be conspicuous," or "to fall onto a surface."

10 "die einzige möglichkeit / in Deutschland / subversiv zu sein / ist / nicht zu funktionieren /…"

11 "so wurde ich / zum nomaden / in sprachen / und halte lebenswache / zwischen den worten."

12 Bill Ashcroft *et al. The Empire Writes Back: Theory and Practice in Post-Colonial Literatures*, 71.

13 *The Empire Writes Back*, 66.

14 Çirak, *Vogel*, 16–17.

15 "Sommeraustausch und Erholung am Meer / dort bekommen wir Sonne viel / und Wärme viel / und noch mehr / noch mehr fürs gute Geld."

16 "der Handel reibt sich die Hände / eline sağlik."

17 "der smartverpackte bankangestellte."

18 "der schalterbleiche postbeamte."

19 "der traditionelle strafzettelverteiler."

20 "dienstlich ruhig korrekt gelassen wie immer."

21 "mit zucht und ordnung lebt der tag erst auf."

22 "kronk wääre im Uslond / ha des mueß mr doch wisse / do wurd mr doch immer hinde un vorne beschisse"

23 "deutsch-sein, meinte ein Freund, heißt / goethe in sich zu spüren"

24 "Oh pardon … / Ich vergaß, / daß ich in Deutschland bin."

25 "Ein Aufwachen, / wie man nur in Deutschland aufwachen kann. / Wie man in Deutschland aufwachen muß. / Wie man gezwungen wird, / in Deutschland aufzuwachen. / Wie man gezwungen wird, / in Deutschland aufzuwachen, / wenn man in diesem Land geboren wurde, / aber nie dazugehören durfte."

26 "Feuergeschmack auf den Zungen. / Der Geruch ist ein Feuer, / das man gelegt hat. / Immer legt. / Selbstbewacht. / Bloße Worte. / Feuer. / Das betrunkene Gelächter der Brandstifter. / Das betrunkene Gelächter der Gerechten, / der Immergerechten."

27 "ein tod wie Auschwitz immernoch / noch-nicht/ was kommt / menschendeutschland du warum? läßt du zu? / läßt dir zu? / den todesort die flucht das mal / erneut auf dieser stirn – ... / das deutsche alphabet / das anders lauten könnte / heißt volk und volk so völkisch volk / beginnt mit H mit H wie M / in Hoyerswerda Hünxe Mölln."

28 "als die MAUER fiel / war ich nicht darauf gefaßt / als die MAUER fiel / mußte ich mich fassen / als die MAUER fiel / war ich fassungslos froh / als die MAUER fiel / und die national-hymne / angestimmt wurde / wußte ich / als die MAUER fiel / die MAUER steht."

29 Çirak, *Fremde Flügel auf eigener Schulter* [*Foreign Wings on One's Own Shoulder*], 39.

30 "Grüß Gott sagen sie / aber was geschieht / wenn ich ihn nicht treffe / grüß dich selber denke ich / und weiß / mein Gruß wird keinem fehlen / Ich grüße sagt der Papst fast fehlerfrei / über Satellit an jedem Ostern / in Sprachen der meisten Welt / man hört ihn selbst noch / in der wenigsten / Grüß noch einmal Papst / nach innen / jene deren Mützen nach außen gewendet / an Tagen die keine Feiertage."

31 "Der eine muß / und der andere frei entwilligte Soldat / das sind die Hampelmänner der Nation / die Schnur das ist der Staat / der lange alte Zopf vorm Vaterland / und die Hände die an dieser Schnur / mal im fummeln nur spielen / mal kurz daran erziehen / und ab und zu auch lange daran zerren / das sind die großkopferten Oberhäupte / Dummköpfe die Dummbeine in Bewegung setzen"

32 Çirak, *Flügel*, 76.

33 Çirak, *Flügel*, 82–3.

34 "Was kann ich denn dafür / daß ich schon Europäerin bin / eine von der satten und matten / der verwestlichten Sorte / eine die noch nicht ums Überleben betteln muß / eine die sich überlegen überlegt / wie die Welt die restliche / noch zu retten ist / eine die sich nicht verstecken kann / wenn sie kommen um zu fordern / etwa / gib mir dein tägliches Brot / und gib mir dein nächtliches Lager / gib mir etwas von dir ab."

35 Both poems are published in *Vogel auf dem Rücken eines Elefanten.*

36 "Weil man weiß, daß auch Brücken ein Ende haben / braucht man sich beim Übergang nicht zu beeilen / doch auf Brücken ist es am kältesten."

37 "Also würde ich am liebsten japanisch aufwachen auf einem Bodenbett in Räumen mit transparenten Scheintüren. Dann würde ich gerne englisch frühstücken, danach mit fremder Gleichgültigkeit chinesisch arbeiten, fleißig und eifrig. Am liebsten möchte französisch essen und tierisch satt römisch baden, gerne will ich bayrisch wandern und afrikanisch tanzen. Am liebsten würde ich russische Geduld besitzen und mein Geld nicht amerikanisch verdienen müssen. Ach, wie möchte ich indisch einschlafen als Vogel auf dem Rücken eines Elefanten und türkisch träumen vom Bosporus."

38 "Identitätskrise / sagt man / der '2. Generation' nach / Identitätskrise / Wie kann man / von einer Krise sprechen / wenn es niemals / eine / Identität / für uns gab"

39 "Ja / in meinem spanischen Reisepaß steht / folgende Nummer: / EC00835133 / in Deutschland gezeugt / aus Spanien importiert / seither trage ich / eine unsichtbare Tätowierung / einzusehen / in irgendeinem Archiv / Zahlen sind doch völkerverbindend / und ich darf existieren / seit wir / diese sonderbare Mischung sind / aus Kennummer und gültigem Stempel / dürfen wir hier leben / Danke / wie hätte ich sonst jemals erfahren / wer ich bin / EC00835133."

40 See Werner Schiffauer, "Europäische Ängste: Metaphern und Phantasmen im Diskurs der Neuen Rechten in Europa." This essay is included in Schiffauers collection of essays *Fremde in der Stadt: Zehn Essays über Kultur und Differenz.*

41 Çirak, *Fremde Flügel auf eigener Schulter.*

42 *The Empire Writes Back,* 38.

43 *The Empire Writes Back,* 38.

CHAPTER FOUR

1 Hartwig Isernhagen, "Literature-Language-Country: The Preservation of Difference and the Possibility of Relation," 86.

2 Emily Hicks, "Deterritorialization and Border Writing," 47, 49.

3 See Gloria Anzaldúa, *Borderlands/La Frontera.*

4 As I have shown in chapter 3, Zehra Çirak shares Gloria Anzaldúa's dream of a world that not only tolerates the transgression of borders but also valorizes it.

5 The English word home does not capture the values connoted in the peculiarly German concept of "Heimat." Implying a sense of shared history of a specific location by an ethnically homogenous group, the term "Heimat" signifies far more than "homeland."

6 Thomas Nolden claims that "many of the texts written by female German Jewish authors are oriented towards intimate genres, such as letter- or diary-writing," "Contemporary German Jewish Literature," 88.

7 "Hier bin ich gelandet vom dreifachen Todessprung ohne Netz: vom Osten in den Westen, von Deutschland nach Frankreich und aus der Assimilation mitten in das Thora-Judentum hinein. " *Roman von einem Kinde*, 111.

8 "Immer Streit, immer über dasselbe: über Hitler über Stalin über die Deutschen über die Russen über die Juden über den Krieg über den Osten über den Westen und über unsere Eltern, vor allem über unsere Eltern." *Roman von einem Kinde*, 55.

9 "Es ist dieser Konflikt, diese Überspanntheit, vor der ich weggelaufen bin. Hier, in Frankreich, geht mich alles viel weniger an, ich bin nur ein Zuschauer, ein Gast, eine Fremde. Das hat mich von der unerträglichen Nähe zu Deutschland befreit." "Von den Legenden der Kindheit, dem Weggehen und der Wiederkehr," 39.

10 "Nun weiß ich, was es heißt, fremd zu sein. Dieses vage schon immer anwesende Gefühl hatte sich hier in eine Wirklichkeit verwandelt." *Roman von einem Kinde*, 114.

11 Anzaldúa, 3.

12 See Marilyn Sibley Fries, "Text as Locus, Inscription as Identity: On Barbara Honigmann's *Roman von einem Kinde*."

13 Anat Feinberg, "Abiding in a Haunted Land: The Issue of Heimat in Contemporary German-Jewish Writing," 165.

14 Irena Klepfisz is a Polish-born Jewish American poet and Holocaust survivor who writes bilingual poetry in English and Yiddish.

15 Jane Hedley, "Nepantilist Poetics: Narrative and Cultural Identity in the Mixed-Language Writings of Irena Klepfisz and Gloria Anzaldúa," 37.

16 Hedley, 39.

17 Julia Kristeva defines the *semiotic*, as distinguished from the *symbolic* as follows: "The semiotic activity, which introduces wandering or fuzziness into language and, *a fortiori*, into poetic language is, from a synchronic point of view, a mark of the workings of drives (appropriation/rejection, orality/anality, love/hate, life/

death) and, from a diachronic point of view, stems from the archaisms of the semiotic body. Before recognizing itself as identical in a mirror and, consequently, as signifying, this body is dependent vis-à-vis the mother. At the same time instinctual and maternal, semiotic processes prepare the future speaker for entrance into meaning and signification (the symbolic)." "From one Identity to an Other," 136. "From one Identity to an Other" is a chapter in Kristeva's *Desire in Language: A Semiotic Approach.*

18 "Es ist schön, daß man zuerst so lange stumm miteinander lebt und erst langsam zusammen ein Wort nach dem anderen findet und das ganze Leben buchstabieren lernt." *Roman von einem Kinde,* 19.

19 "Einmal hatte ich einen Traum. Da war ich mit all den anderen in Auschwitz. Und in dem Traum dachte ich: Endlich habe ich meinen Platz im Leben gefunden." *Roman von einem Kinde,* 28.

20 "Jerusalem wäre gut, New York wäre gut, London wäre gut, sonstwo wäre gut, aber Deutschland ist nicht mehr gut für Juden. Hier kann man nichts mehr lernen, also hat es keinen Sinn zu bleiben." *Roman von einem Kinde,* 94.

21 Like her protagonist, Renan Demirkan was born in Ankara, grew up in Germany and works as an actor.

22 Renan Demirkan. *Schwarzer Tee mit drei Stück Zucker,* 17. Henceforth cited in the text as *Schwarzer Tee.*

23 "Ich bin Kosmopolitin!" *Schwarzer Tee,* 57.

24 "Improvisiertes Überleben" and "Nach-der-Stechuhr-Funktionieren." *Schwarzer Tee,* 137–8.

25 Leslie Adelson, "Migrants' Literature," 385. In her argument Adelson draws attention to the fact that German colonialists of the late nineteenth and early twentieth centuries "read their extensive bureaucratic administration as a sign of German superiority over native peoples in Africa and the South Pacific." "Migrants' Literature," 385.

26 Saliha Scheinhardt is the most prolific and probably the most widely read German Turkish woman writer. Her early novels *Frauen, die sterben, ohne daß sie gelebt hätten* [*Women Who Die without Having Lived*], *Drei Zypressen* [*Three Cypresses*], and *Und die Frauen weinten Blut* [*And the Women Wept Blood*] intend to appeal to the German readers' emotions in order to heighten their awareness of the Turkish women's suffering at the hands of brutal husbands.

27 See Marilya Veteto-Conrad's chapter on the writing by German Turkish women.

28 "Hör zu: Wir holen das Berglein aus dem Dorf meiner Großeltern und stellen es an den Rhein ... Dann basteln wir einen maisgelben Baldachin mit Sternen und machen deinen Platz daraus. Mit bunten Kelims aus der Türkei, weichen Federkissen aus Österreich und kuscheligen Plüschtieren aus Deutschland bauen wir das schönste Himmelbett auf Erden ... Wenn wir alle zusammen singen, ist es kein trauriges Lied. Anschließend paddeln wir alle gemeinsam zum Museum hinüber und sehen uns die Andy-Warhol-Ausstellung an. Wenn dir das nicht gefällt, drehen wir alles um: tragen den Rhein, den Dom, die Altstadt, das Museum und die Speckpfannkuchen ins Dorf meiner Großeltern und lesen dort auf dem Berglein an den Wochenenden Gedichte von Goethe und Heine." *Schwarzer Tee*, 120–1.
29 "Urhaftes Stöhnen." *Schwarzer Tee*, 36.
30 Maxim Biller and Rafael Seligmann, for example, in their impatience with both Jewish and non-Jewish taboos, use Yiddish expressions in their texts to caricature and subvert stereotypes of the Jew.
31 Guy Stern, "Barbara Honigmann: A Preliminary Assessment," 335.
32 Sander Gilman, "Jewish Writers in Contemporary Germany: The Dead Author Speaks."
33 Gilman, "Jewish Writers," 315.
34 Gilman, "Jewish Writers," 316.
35 Honigmann, "On My Great-Grandfather," 514.
36 Teraoka, *"Gastarbeiterliteratur,"* 294.

CHAPTER FIVE

1 Eva Hoffman's text appeared in German translation in 1993 and is widely read in Germany.
2 Dan Diner contends that the Holocaust defines the identities of both Germans and Jews and has become some kind of "communality of opposites." "Negative Symbiose: Deutsche und Juden nach Auschwitz," 9.
3 See also Maxim Biller, "Philip Roth: Die Zeit der Ungeheuer ist vorbei" ["Philip Roth: The Time of the Monsters is Past"] in his collection of essays *Die Tempojahre* [*The Tempo Years*] (1991), in which he identifies other major differences between postwar German Jewish and Jewish American discourse.
4 Arnold Rampersad, "Biography, Autobiography, and Afro-American Culture," 9.

5 "Die Tür wird luftdicht abgeschlossen: Schma Israel," "Ich hatte einen deutschen Paß, aber eine Deutsche war ich nicht," "Fünf Jahre lebte ich mit ihnen: Es ist genug."

6 "Wo beginnen Erinnerungen?" Lea Fleischmann, *Dies ist nicht mein Land*, 8.

7 "Ich hörte von Juden, die ihre Gräber selber ausheben mußten, bevor sie erschossen wurden, ich hörte von Müttern, denen man die Kinder entrissen und vor ihren Augen erschlagen hatte, ich hörte von Vergasung, bevor ich wußte, was Gas ist, ich hörte von Hunden, die man auf Menschen gehetzt hatte, ich hörte von Kindern, die man lebendig in Feuergruben geworfen hatte." *Dies ist nicht mein Land*, 23.

8 "Fünf Jahre lebte meine Mutter unter den Deutschen, und fünf Jahre lebte ich mit ihnen. Es ist genug." *Dies ist nicht mein Land*, 205.

9 Lea Fleischmann worked as a teacher in Wiesbaden and in Offenbach between 1973 and 1978.

10 "In meiner jüdischen Isolation." *Dies ist nicht mein Land*, 65.

11 "Wir mußten unsere Gräber selber ausheben, er [Jesus] starb ohne Widerstand, und wir ließen uns widerstandslos hinmetzeln." *Dies ist nicht mein Land*, 173.

12 "Anders als die 'Alt-68er' und die postmodernen 'Neonkids' haben die 78er keine politisch oder kulturell griffige Symbolik entwickelt, die sie auf Anhieb identifizierbar machte ... Es ist das kontingente Merkmal dieser Generation, daß sie biographisch mit einem Bein in der Geschichte und mit dem anderen in einer vermeintlich zukunftslosen Gegenwart steht." Reinhard Mohr, *Zaungäste: Die Generation, die nach der Revolte kam*, 10–11. Richard Chaim Schneider refers to Mohr's book and identifies with the "78er Generation." *Zwischen Welten*, 169.

13 "Micha Brumlik, Henryk M. Broder, Lea Fleischmann, Michael Wolffsohn und wie die jüdischen Galionsfiguren der deutschen Medien alle heißen mögen, sie gehen allmählich auf die 50 zu. Wir aber, die wir bald 40 werden, scheinen stumm zu sein." Richard Chaim Schneider, *Zwischen Welten*, 169.

14 "Fassbinder," "Deplazierte Personen," "Hellas," "Deutschland," "Israel," and "Höre Israel." The title of the last chapter seems to allude to Erich Fried's volume of poems *Höre, Israel!* (1974), in which he accuses Israel of persecuting the Palestinians.

15 "Den kulturellen und emotionalen Hintergrund." *Zwischen Welten*, 11.

16 "Sie hätte keinen Sinn mehr." *Zwischen Welten*, 292.

17 In "Rainer Werner Fassbinder's *Garbage, the City and Death*: Renewed Antagonisms in the Complex Relationship between Jews and Germans in the Federal Republic of Germany," Andrei S. Markovits observes that seven attempts were made between 1976 and 1985 by various Frankfurt theatres to have the play performed.

18 See Markovits.

19 Ruth K. Angress, "A 'Jewish Problem' in German Postwar Fiction," 227–28. Angress explains that "in their defense in *Die Zeit*, both Zwerenz and Fassbinder point out that Jewish speculators were active and successful in Frankfurt and did harm the city." "A 'Jewish Problem,'" (229). Andrei S. Markovits, however, comes to Zwerenz's defence: "Zwerenz's main Jewish character, Abraham Mauerstamm, may appear as somewhat of an equivocating and weak figure, but he is certainly devoid of any evil intentions. Moreover, Zwerenz's world is populated by explicitly 'good Jews,' such as the character based on Fritz Bauer, the prosecutor in Frankfurt's Auschwitz trial of the 1960s." "Rainer Werner Fassbinder's *Garbage, the City and Death*," 7–8. Markovits also points out that Zwerenz "objected to Fassbinder's creation of the 'Rich Jew,' whereupon Fassbinder promised to rewrite the role calling the new character the 'Rich Poor Jew' thereby trying to convey that after Auschwitz even the richest Jew remained poor as well." "Rainer Werner Fassbinder's *Garbage, the City and Death*," 8. Fassbinder, however, never did change this character.

20 See Ruth Angress.

21 Cilly Kugelmann points out that "in the 1987 discussions about anti-Semitism or about the postwar relationship between Jews and Germans, the bitterly contested semantic problem of whether the binary opposition Jew/German can legitimately be used was often debated. Non-Jews in the discussion took the citizens' position, according to which every German citizen is also a German. They therefore perceive the Jew/German distinction the Jews have introduced as a provocative separatism in the tradition of the Nürnberg Laws." "'Tell Them in America We're Still Alive!': The Jewish Community in the Federal Republic," 129.

22 "Die Fassbinder-Affäre hat mich aus einem mir selbst verordneten Dornröschenschlaf wachgeküßt." *Zwischen Welten*, 59.

23 "Jude sein in Deutschland wurde zur Manifestation des Fremdseins." *Zwischen Welten*, 59.

24 "Ganz leise in mir gab es eine Stimme, die entsetzt reagierte auf die Bilder, die da gezeigt wurden: Ein älterer Herr erzählte dem Fernseh-reporter in schlechtem Deutsch, wie er im KZ gelitten hatte, junge Juden sangen idiotenstolz vor laufender Kamera 'Am Jisrael Chai' – das jüdische Volk lebt. Unbehagen breitete sich in mir aus, damit wollte ich nichts zu tun haben. Ich schämte mich, mit ihnen in einen Topf geworfen zu werden. Ich bin nicht wie diese, ich habe mich emanzipiert, ich weiß, wie man sich wahrhaftig als Demokrat ver-hält ... Ich kann sogar richtig Deutsch sprechen. Ich bin kein Stetl-Jude, ich schaue nicht aus wie ein Jude. Ich bin groß, stark, habe keine gebogene Nase, kann mich benehmen." *Zwischen Welten*, 34.

25 Schneider explains that East European Jews followed religious tra-dition to a much higher degree than pre-Holocaust German Jews. He also explains that his religious education was not consistent. Although his family used to light candles on Friday night, his father recited the Kiddush, and they had gefilte fish for dinner, they sat down to watch TV afterwards.

26 "Grenze zwischen Gefilte Fisch und Weißwürsten." *Zwischen Welten*, 97.

27 Cilly Kugelmann, "'Tell them in America We're Still Alive!': The Jewish Community in the Federal Republic," 134.

28 Kugelmann, 134.

29 "Es galt, die wichtigsten Bastionen westlicher Kultur auf einmal zu erobern: Athen und Rom und Berlin." *Zwischen Welten*, 116.

30 "Wenn unser Sohn im deutschen Gymnasium besteht, dann gehört er auch zur Herrenrasse, er ist dann kein Untermensch. Wieder so eine widersprüchliche Aussage: Wehre dich, wir Juden sind heute auch etwas wert, werde deutsch, dann gehörst du erst wirklich zur Her-renrasse, aber assimiliere dich auf keinen Fall." *Zwischen Welten*, 128.

31 Henry L. Feingold, "*Bildung*: Was It Good for the Jews?" 60.

32 Feingold, 60.

33 "Ich hielt mich jetzt fest an ihm, an diesem anderen Deutschland, an das ich doch so gerne glauben wollte, dem ich mich so zuge-hörig fühlte." *Zwischen Welten*, 177.

34 Sander L. Gilman, "Jewish Writers in Contemporary Germany: The Dead Author Speaks," 336.

35 Gilman, "Jewish Writers," 336.

36 "'Du kennst die Bücher der Gojim ganz hervorragend. Aber die Bücher deines Volkes kennst du nicht halb so gut.'" *Zwischen Welten*, 149.

37 Jews are exempt from military service in the Federal Republic.

38 "Denn mein Zwiespalt wurde unermeßlich, als ich am Schalter meinen deutschen Paß erhielt, ihn aufschlug und auf der ersten Seite die Zeile las: 'Der Inhaber diese Passes ist Deutscher.'" *Zwischen Welten*, 171.

39 "Die geistige und kulturelle Kluft zwischen Diaspora und Israel wird immer größer. Israel liegt in der Levante ... Und damit wird es uns europäischen Juden immer fremder." *Zwischen Welten*, 228.

40 See Introduction, 15.

41 Jack Zipes, "The Contemporary German Fascination for Things Jewish: Toward a Jewish Minor Culture," 17.

CHAPTER SIX

1 Henceforth cited in the text as *Verschwinden* and as *Mondsichel*.

2 Mary Louise Pratt, *Imperial Eyes: Travel Writing and Transculturation*, 7.

3 Rana Kabbani, *Europe's Myths of Orient: Devise and Rule*, 122, 128.

4 Edward W. Said, *Orientalism*, 4.

5 Said, 19.

6 Donna K. Heizer, *Jewish-German Identity in the Orientalist Literature of Else Lasker-Schüler, Friedrich Wolf, and Franz Werfel*, 7. The German word "Orient" generally refers to the Middle East and Northern Africa and, unlike its English and French counterparts, does not include the Far East.

7 Heizer, 7.

8 See Donna K. Heizer, *German-Jewish Identity*, 7. See also Andrea Fuchs-Sumiyoshi, *Orientalismus in der deutschen Literatur*, 12.

9 See Nazire Akbulut, *Das Türkenbild in der neueren deutschen Literatur 1970–1990*, 100.

10 Arlene Akiko Teraoka, *East, West, and Others*, 5.

11 "Du wirst schön sein, du wirst schön sein!" *Verschwinden*, 69.

12 "Manchmal verstehe ich dich nicht, sagte Sevim, du kennst uns, du lebst mit uns, du interessierst dich für alles, was uns betrifft, das heißt, was uns betroffen hat, du sprichst unsere Sprache, du weißt über unsere Geschichte Bescheid und trotzdem schaust du nicht wirklich um dich, nimmst vieles nicht wahr, was um dich her vorgeht. Du hast einen eigenen Blick dafür entwickelt, was von früher her noch an uns ist, aber das, was neu an uns ist, interessiert dich nicht." *Verschwinden*, 142.

13 "Zweifel an der Sprache" and "Verzweifeln an der Sprache." See
Barbara Frischmuth quoted in Donald G. Daviau, "Neue Entwick-
lungen in der modernen österreichischen Prosa: Die Werke von
Barbara Frischmuth," 179.

14 "Ich sah einer Sprache zu, wie sie sich änderte, aber der Versuch,
mit ihr Schritt zu halten, brachte nichts als Niederlagen." *Verschwinden*, 38.

15 "Ich hatte Schwierigkeiten, Sätze zu bilden, und fiel in das Stadium
der ersten Wochen zurück, in denen ich mich nur mühsam verstän-
digen konnte, obwohl ich schon Bücher in der Sprache gelesen
hatte." *Verschwinden*, 24–5.

16 "Konsumgesellschaft, Gehaltserhöhungen und Profitraten, Alltags-
trott und enfremdete [sic] Arbeit." *Mondsichel*, 11.

17 "Jetzt kam ihr auch noch ein Goethezitat in den Kopf, dessen
Aussage überhaupt nicht zur Situation paßte. Überhaupt, was hatte
sie nicht alles über die Türkei gelesen!" *Mondsichel*, 10.

18 "'Ich verstehe eines nicht,' sagte Berrin, 'du fährst fast jedes Jahr
für zwei oder drei Monate in die Türkei, hast viel gesehen und
kennst die Ansichten deiner Freunde über die politischen Verhält-
nisse in ihrem Land. Das sollte dir eigentlich helfen, über die
Geschichte von Yesilçai hinwegzukommen.'" *Mondsichel*, 93.

19 Marilya Veteto-Conrad, *Finding a Voice: Identity and the Works of
German-Language Turkish Writers in the Federal Republic of Germany to
1990*, 60.

20 Veteto-Conrad, 64.

21 See Annette Wierschke, *Schreiben als Selbstbehauptung: Kulturkonflikt
und Identität in den Werken von Aysel Özakin, Alev Tekinay und Emine
Sevgi Özdamar*. The English translation of *Die Preisvergabe* appeared
in 1988.

22 "Der Herr war vor den Kopf gestoßen und wandte sich diskret ab.
Eine Dame aus Europa hatte er sich etwas anders vorgestellt. Hatte
nicht im entferntesten damit gerechnet, einem widerspenstigen
Wesen mit muskulösen Armen und Beinen zu begegnen, dessen
ausgeblichenes, offen getragenes Haar genauso zerzaust aussah wie
die Mähne des Pferdes." *Mondsichel*, 16.

23 "Während das Abscheuliche an Mehmets Mord ausführlich und für
den Leser realistisch beschrieben wird, adaptiert die Erzählerin für
Schengüls Tat die Mythenwelt." Nazire Akbulut, *Das Türkenbild in
der neueren deutschen Literatur 1970–1990*, 167.

24 Barbara G. Walker. *The Woman's Dictionary of Symbols and Sacred Objects*, 345.

25 See Georg Pichler, "'Seltsam, daß es mir so wenig ausmacht, nicht anzukommen.' Heimat und Fremde bei Barbara Frischmuth," 66.

CHAPTER SEVEN

1 Feridun Zaimoglu was born in Turkey in 1964 and emigrated to Germany with his parents when he was five years old. He lives in Kiel and is one of the founders of the literary magazine ARGOS.

2 "Weinerliche, sich anbiedernde und öffentlich geförderte 'Gastarbeiterliteratur.'" Feridun Zaimoglu, *Kanak Sprak*, 11.

3 "Die Kanaken suchen keine kulturelle Verankerung. Sie möchten sich weder im Supermarkt der Identitäten bedienen, noch in einer egalitären Herde von Heimatvertriebenen aufgehen. Sie haben eine eigene innere Prägung und ganz klare Vorstellungen von Selbstbestimmung. Sie bilden die eigentliche Generation X, der Individuation und Ontogenese verweigert worden sind." *Kanak Sprak* 12–13.

4 See Anna K. Kuhn, "Bourgeois Ideology and the (Mis)Reading of Günter Wallraff's *Ganz Unten*."

5 "Meine gespielte Torheit machte mich schlauer, eröffnete mir Einblicke in die Borniertheit und Eiseskälte einer Gesellschaft, die sich für so gescheit, souverän, endgültig und gerecht hält. Ich war der Narr, dem man die Wahrheit unverstellt sagt." Günter Wallraff, *Ganz Unten*, 12.

6 "Ausländer, kräftig, sucht Arbeit, egal was, auch Schwerst- u. Drecksarb., auch für wenig Geld." *Ganz Unten*, 11.

7 Aysel Özakin, "Ali hinter den Spiegeln," 6.

8 Özakin, 7.

9 "Sicher, ich war nicht wirklich ein Türke. Aber man muß täuschen und sich verstellen, um die Wahrheit herauszufinden." *Ganz Unten*, 12.

10 See Anna K. Kuhn, 198.

11 "Daß diese Figur alles hochwirbelt, nicht damit einverstanden ist und nicht alles schluckt." *Ganz Unten*, 428.

12 "Ich stecke nicht nur ein. Ich gebe auch zurück. Das ist ein Widerstandspotential von unten." *Ganz Unten*, 428.

13 "Innerhalb der Rolle zu leben, ist gleichzeitig Spiel, ein ganz befreiendes Moment, viel intensiver und authentischer. Es ist für

mich immer wieder eine Suche nach Identität, eine Möglichkeit, mir meiner selbst bewußt zu werden, und es ist auch meine Neugierde." *Ganz Unten,* 428.

14 See Introduction, note 32.

15 "'Kanak-Sprak,' eine Art Creol oder Rotwelsch mit geheimen Codes und Zeichen. Ihr Reden ist dem Free-Style-Sermon im Rap verwandt, dort wie hier spricht man aus einer Pose heraus." Feridun Zaimoglu, *Kanak Sprak,* 13.

16 Michael Quinn, "'Never shoulda been let out the penitentiary': Gangsta Rap and the Struggle over Racial Identity," 71.

17 Christoph Ribbat, "Borrowed Beats and Native Tongues: Multicultural Rap in Germany," 14.

18 Quoted in Ribbat, 16.

19 See Ribbat.

20 Salaam ya, Mitume, "The Aesthetics of Rap," 313.

21 "Wir sind hier allesamt nigger, wir haben unser ghetto, wir schleppen's überall hin, wir dampfen fremdländisch, unser schweiß ist nigger, unser leben ist nigger, die goldketten sind nigger, unsere zinken und unsere fressen und unser eigner stil ist so verdammt nigger, daß wir wie blöde an unsrer haut kratzen, und dabei kapieren wir, daß zum nigger nicht die olle pechhaut gehört, aber zum nigger gehört ne ganze menge anderssein und andres leben." *Kanak Sprak,* 25.

22 "Ich geb dir reinen Stoff. Du bist mein Dealer. Geh und verkauf das Zeug!." *Abschaum,* 184.

23 "Wir wollen uns mit den insignien der blonden übermenschen schmücken. Unser eigener schlechter geschmack kommt uns in die quere und das uns eingeflößte gefühl, daß wir minderwertig sind. Deshalb färben sich viele kümmelmammas ihr haar blond und tragen unsere pop-starletts blaue oder grüne kontaktlinsen. Deshalb giert das turcokid nach einem daimler. Deshalb sticht mancher kümmel zu: er will hart sein wie kruppstahl und aussehen wie ein provinzpopper. Den wechsel vom ackerland zum fließband haben wir nicht verdaut … Solange dieses land uns den wirklichen eintritt verwehrt, werden wir die anomalien und perversionen dieses landes wie ein schwamm aufsaugen und den dreck ausspucken. Die beschmutzten kennen keine *ästhetik.*" *Kanak Sprak,* 113–14.

24 Mikhail Bakhtin, *Rabelais and His World,* 317.

25 Bakhtin, 317.

26 "Nun sitz ich hier und versuch unsere Intellektuellen zu schocken, ich versuch unsere Assimilierten zu erschrecken, hier bestimmte Leute zu faszinieren: Faszination durchs kriminelle Subjekt, Faszination durchs wilde Andere, Faszination für die, die von ganz unten kommen." *Abschaum*, 180.

27 bell hooks, *Outlaw Culture*, 116.

28 hooks, *Outlaw Culture*, 121.

29 "Ich hab mein Arschloch fotografiert und es aufgehängt, weil ich es geil finde." *Abschaum*, 125.

30 In the preface to *Koppstoff* [*Head Stuff*], his most recent book, Zaimoglu points out that at public readings the most frequently made critical comment about his texts was that they present the *Kanaksta* world exclusively from the male point of view. Zaimoglu explains that to make amends he wrote *Koppstoff* as a "female" version of *Kanak Sprak*.

31 Frank Chin, "Come All Ye Asian American Writers of the Real and the Fake," 24.

32 Leslie A. Adelson, "Minor Chords? Migration, Murder, and Multiculturalism," 122.

33 Adelson, "Minor Chords?," 122–3.

34 Adelson, "Minor Chords?," 123.

CONCLUSION

1 Stephen Slemon sees the settler cultures of Australia, Canada, southern Africa, and New Zealand as inhabiting the "Second World." "Fourth World" refers to indigenous peoples colonized in their own countries. "Unsettling the Empire: Resistance Theory for the Second World."

2 Slemon, 233.

3 See Wolfgang Beutin et al. *Deutsche Literatur-Geschichte: Von den Anfängen bis zur Gegenwart*, 601–5.

4 Henry Louis Gates, "Ethnic and Minority' Studies," 298.

5 Stephen Slemon, 235.

6 Jenny Sharpe, "Figures of Colonial Resistance."

7 The same argument needs to be made for German Studies in Canada.

8 Lutz P. Koepnick, "Negotiating Popular Culture: Wenders, Handke, and the Topographies of Cultural Studies," 381.

Works Cited

Ackermann, Irmgard, ed. *Fremde AugenBlicke: Mehrkulturelle Literatur in Deutschland.* Bonn: Inter Nationes 1996

Ackermann, Irmgard and Harald Weinrich, eds. *Eine nicht nur deutsche Literatur: Zur Standortbestimmung der "Ausländerliteratur."* München: Piper 1986

Adelson, Leslie A. "Minor Chords? Migration, Murder, and Multiculturalism." *Wendezeiten/Zeitenwenden: Positionsbestimmungen zur deutschprachigen* Literatur 1945–1995, 115–29. Eds. Robert Weninger and Brigitte Rossbacher. Tübingen: Stauffenburg Verlag 1997

– "Opposing Oppositions: Turkish-German Questions in Contemporary German Studies." *German Studies Review* 17, no. 2 (1994): 305–30

– "Migrants' Literature or German Literature? Torkan's Tufan: *Brief an einen islamischen Bruder.*" *The German Quarterly* 63, no. 3–4 (1990): 382–9

Akbulut, Nazire. *Das Türkenbild in der neueren deutschen Literatur 1970–1990.* Berlin: Verlag Köster 1993

Angress, Ruth K. "A 'Jewish Problem' in German Postwar Fiction." *Modern Judaism* 5, no. 3 (1985): 215–33

Anzaldúa, Gloria. *Borderlands/La Frontera: The New Mestiza.* San Francisco: spinsters/aunt lute 1987

Ashcroft, Bill, Gareth Griffiths, and Helen Tiffin. *The Empire Writes Back: Theory and Practice in Post-Colonial Literatures.* London: Routledge 1989

Bade, Klaus J. "Einwanderung und Gesellschaftspolitik in Deutschland – quo vadis Bundesrepublik?" *Die multikulturelle Herausforderung:*

Menschen über Grenzen – Grenzen über Menschen, 230–53. Ed. Klaus J. Bade. München: Verlag C.H. Beck 1996

Bakhtin, Mikhail. *Rabelais and His World*. Trans. Hélène Iswolsky. Bloomington: Indiana University Press 1988

Becker, Jurek. "Die Wiedervereinigung der deutschen Literatur." *The German Quarterly* 63, no. 3–4 (1990): 59–66

Bender, Peter. "Vereinigen können sich nur Gleiche: Über die dreifache Enteignung der Ostdeutschen." *Merkur* 52, no. 1 (1998): 73–9

Beutin, Wolfgang et al. *Deutsche Literatur-Geschichte: Von den Anfängen bis zur Gegenwart*. Stuttgart: Metzler 1994

Biller, Maxim. *Die Tempojahre*. München: Deutscher Taschenbuch Verlag 1991

Biondi, Franco. *Abschied der zerschellten Jahre: Novelle*. Kiel: Neuer Malik Verlag 1984

– "Die Fremde wohnt in der Sprache." *Eine nicht nur deutsche Literatur: Zur Standortbestimmung der "Ausländerliteratur,"* 25–32. Eds. Irmgard Ackermann and Harald Weinrich. München: Piper 1986

Biondi, Franco and Rafik Schami. Unter Mitarbeit von Jusuf Naoum and Suleman Taufiq. "Literatur der Betroffenheit: Bemerkungen zur Gastarbeiterliteratur." *Zu Hause in der Fremde: Ein bundesdeutsches Ausländer-Lesebuch*, 124–36. Ed. Christian Schaffernicht. Fischerhude: Atelier im Bauernhaus 1981

Blaber, Ronald and Marvin Gilman. *Roguery: The Picaresque Tradition in Australian, Canadian and Indian Fiction*. Springwood, New South Wales: Butterfly Books 1990

Bodemann, Y. Michal. "A Reemergence of German Jewry?" *Reemerging Jewish Culture in Germany: Life and Literature since 1989*, 46–61. Eds. Sander L. Gilman and Karen Remmler. New York: New York University Press 1994

Boetcher Joeres, Ruth-Ellen and Elizabeth Mittman, eds. "An Introductory Essay." *The Politics of the Essay: Feminist Perspectives*, 12–20. Bloomington: Indiana University Press 1993

Borneman, John. "Time-Space Compression and the Continental Divide in German Subjectivity." *New Formations* 21 (1994): 102–18

Brady, John. "Public and Private: Immigrants and the Search for a Common Political Language." *Bad Subjects: Political Education for Everyday Life*, 244–47. New York: New York University Press 1998

Brokoph-Mauch, Gudrun. "Die Begegnung mit dem Orient in Barbara Frischmuths Roman 'Das Verschwinden des Schattens in der Sonne.'" *Akten des VIII Internationalen Germanisten-Kongresses: Begegnung mit dem*

'Fremden.' *Grenzen, Traditionen, Vergleiche*, 85–90. Ed. Eijiro Iwasaki. München: iudicium 1991

Brussig, Thomas. *Helden wie wir*. Berlin: Volk & Welt 1995

Brydon, Diana and Helen Tiffin. *Decolonising Fictions*. Sydney: Dangaroo Press 1993

Canetti, Elias. *Die Stimmen von Marrakesch: Aufzeichnungen nach einer Reise*. Regensburg: Carl Hanser Verlag 1967

Chambers, Ross. *Room for Maneuver: Reading (the) Oppositional (in) Narrative*. Chicago: The University of Chicago Press 1991

Chin, Frank. "Come All Ye Asian American Writers of the Real and the Fake." *The Big Aiiieeeee! An Anthology of Chinese American and Japanese American Literature*, 1–31. Eds. Jeffery Paul Chan, Frank Chin, L.F. Inada, and Shawn Wong. New York: Meridian 1991

Çirak, Zehra. *Fremde Flügel auf eigener Schulter: Gedichte*. Köln: Kiepenheuer & Witsch 1994

– *Vogel auf dem Rücken eines Elefanten: Gedichte*. Köln: Kiepenheuer & Witsch 1991

Daviau, Donald G. "Neuere Entwicklungen in der modernen österreichischen Prosa: Die Werke von Barbara Frischmuth." *Modern Austrian Literature* 13, no. 1 (1980): 177–216

Deleuze, Gilles and Félix Guattari. *Kafka: Toward a Minor Literature*. Trans. Dana Polan. Minneapolis: University of Minnesota Press 1986

Demirkan, Renan. *Schwarzer Tee mit drei Stück Zucker*. Köln: Kiepenheuer & Witsch, 1991

– "Die Brücke im Januskopf: Vom Altwerden in einem ungastlichen Land." *Deutsche Türken/Türk Almanlar: Das Ende der Geduld/Sabrin sonu*, 79–83. Eds. Claus Leggewie and Zafer Şenocak. Hamburg: Rowohlt 1993

Deutsches Ausländerrecht: AusländerG und DV; AsylverfahrensG; ArbeitserlaubnisVO; AusländerzentralregisterG; Aufenthaltsgesetz/EWG mit Novelle November 1997. München: Verlag C.H. Beck 1998

Diner, Dan. "Negative Symbiose: Deutsche und Juden nach Auschwitz." *Babylon* 1 (1986): 9–20

Dümcke, Wolfgang and Fritz Vilmar, eds. *Kolonialisierung der DDR: Kritische Analysen und Alternativen des Einigungsprozesses*. Münster: Agenda Verlag 1995

Emmerich, Wolfgang. "Status melancholicus. Zur Transformation der Utopie in der DDR-Literatur." *Literatur in der DDR: Rückblicke*, 232–45. Eds. Heinz Ludwig Arnold and Frauke Meyer-Gosau. München: Edition Text + Kritik 1991

Feinberg, Anat. "Abiding in a Haunted Land: The Issue of Heimat in Contemporary German-Jewish Writing." *New German Critique* 70 (1997): 161–81

Feingold, Henry L. *"Bildung*: Was It Good for the Jews?" *The German-Jewish Legacy in America 1938–1988: From Bildung to the Bill of Rights*, 57–61. Ed. Abraham J. Peck. Detroit: Wayne State University Press 1989

Ferguson, Russell. "Introduction: Invisible Center." *Out There: Marginalization and Contemporary Cultures*, 9–14. Eds. Russell Ferguson, Martha Gever, Trinh T. Minh-ha, and Cornel West. New York: MIT Press 1990

Fleischmann, Lea. *Dies ist nicht mein Land: Eine Jüdin verläßt die Bundesrepublik*. München: Wilhelm Heyne Verlag 1992

Flynn, Elizabeth A. "Gender and Reading." *Gender and Reading: Essays on Readers, Texts, and Contexts*, 267–88. Ed. Elizabeth A. Flynn. Baltimore: Johns Hopkins University Press 1986

Foley, Barbara. "Fact, Fiction, Fascism: Testimony and Mimesis in Holocaust Narratives." *Comparative Literature* 34, no. 4 (1982): 330–60

Foucault, Michel. "Of Other Spaces." *Diacritics* 16, no.1 (1986): 22–7

Fries, Marilyn Sibley. "Text as Locus, Inscription as Identity: On Barbara Honigmann's *Roman von einem Kinde*." *Studies in Twentieth Century Literature* 14, no. 2 (1990): 175–93

Frischmuth, Barbara. *Das Verschwinden des Schattens in der Sonne*. Frankfurt/Main Suhrkamp 1973

Fuchs-Sumiyoshi, Andrea. *Orientalismus in der deutschen Literatur*. Hildesheim: Georg Olms Verlag 1984

Gates, Henry Louis Jr.: "'Ethnic and Minority' Studies." *Introduction to Scholarship in Modern Languages and Literatures*, 288–302. Ed. Joseph Gibaldi. New York: The Modern Language Association of America 1992

Gilman, Sander L. *Jews in Today's German Culture*. Bloomington: Indiana University Press 1995

– "Jewish Writers in Contemporary Germany: The Dead Author Speaks." *Anti-Semitism in Times of Crisis*, 311–42. Eds. Sander L. Gilman and Steven T. Katz. New York: New York University Press 1991

– "German Reunification and the Jews." *New German Critique* 52 (1991): 173–91

Glaser, Hermann. "The Future Requires an Origin: East-West German Identity, the Opportunities and Difficulties of Cultural Politics." *Cultural Transformations in the New Germany: American and German Perspectives*, 64–80. Eds. Friederike Eigler and Peter C. Pfeiffer. Columbia, South Carolina: Camden House 1993

Gunew, Sneja. "Denaturalizing Cultural Nationalism: Multicultural Readings of 'Australia.'" *Nation and Narration*, 99–120. Ed. Homi K. Bhabha. London: Routledge 1993

– "Beyond the Echo: Migrant Writing and Australian Literature." *Displaced Persons*. Eds. K.H. Peterson and A. Rutherford, 54–73. Sydney: Dangaroo Press 1988

Harvey, A.D. "Why the 'Novelle'?" *New German Studies* 16, no. 3 (1990–1991): 159–72

Hedley, Jane. "Nepantilist Poetics: Narrative and Cultural Identity in the Mixed-Language Writings of Irena Klepfisz and Gloria Anzaldúa." *Narrative* 4, no. 1 (1996): 37–54

Heizer, Donna K. *Jewish-German Identity in the Orientalist Literature of Else Lasker-Schüler, Friedrich Wolf, and Franz Werfel*. Columbia, South Carolina: Camden House 1996

Hicks, Emily. "Deterritorialization and Border Writing." *Ethics/Aesthetics: Post-Modern Positions*, 47–58. Eds. Robert Merrill and Pat Wilkinson-Bus. Washington: Maisonneuve Press 1988

Hoffman, Eva. *Lost in Translation: A Life in a New Language*. Harmondsworth: Penguin 1990

Höfer, Konrad, ed. *Johann Peter Eckermann: Gespräche mit Goethe*. Leipzig: Hesse & Becker Verlag 1913

Hoffmann, Lutz. *Die unvollendete Republik: Zwischen Einwanderungsland und deutschem Nationalstaat*. Köln: Papy Rossa Verlag 1992

Holub, Robert C. "Realism, Repetition, Repression: The Nature of Desire in *Romeo und Julia auf dem Dorfe*." *Modern Language Notes* 100, no. 3 (1985): 461–97

Honigmann, Barbara. *Roman von einem Kinde: Sechs Erzählungen*. Hamburg: Luchterhand 1989

– "On My Great-Grandfather, My Grandfather, My Father, and Me." *World Literature Today* 69, no. 3 (1995): 512–16

– "Von den Legenden der Kindheit, dem Weggehen und der Wiederkehr." *Nach der Shoa geboren: Jüdische Frauen in Deutschland*, 35–40. Eds. Jessica Jacoby, Claudia Schoppmann, and Wendy Zena-Henry. Berlin: Elefanten Press 1994

hooks, bell. *Outlaw Culture: Resisting Representations*. New York: Routledge 1994

– *Talking Back: Thinking Feminist, Thinking Black*. Boston: South End Press 1989

Horrocks, David and Eva Kolinsky, eds. *Turkish Culture in German Society Today*. Providence: Berghahn Books 1996

Hüppauf, Bernd. "Moral oder Sprache: DDR-Literatur vor der Moderne." *Literatur in der DDR: Rückblicke*, 220–31. Eds. Heinz Ludwig Arnold and Frauke Meyer-Gosau. München: Edition Text + Kritik 1991

Huyssen, Andreas. "After the Wall: The Failure of German Intellectuals." *New German Critique* 52 (1991): 109–43

Isernhagen, Hartwig. "Literature-Language-Country: The Preservation of Difference and the Possibility of Relation." *Zeitschrift der Gesellschaft für Kanada-Studien* 10, no. 1 (1986): 81–94

Jäger, Andrea. "Schriftsteller-Identität und Zensur: Über die Bedingungen des Schreibens im 'realen Sozialismus.'" *Literatur in der DDR: Rückblicke*, 137–48. Eds. Heinz Ludwig Arnold and Frauke Meyer-Gosau. München: Edition Text + Kritik 1991

Jankowsky, Karen. "'German' Literature Contested: The 1991 Ingeborg-Bachmann-Prize Debate, 'Cultural Diversity,' and Emine Sevgi Özdamar." *The German Quarterly* 70, no. 3 (1997): 261–76

JanMohamed, Abdul R. "Humanism and Minority Literature: Toward a Definition of Counter-hegemonic Discourse." *Boundary 2* 12, no. 3 (1984): 281–99

Jentzsch, Kerstin. *Seit die Götter ratlos sind*. Berlin: Verlag das Neue Berlin 1994

Kabbani, Rana. *Europe's Myths of Orient: Devise and Rule*. London: The Macmillan Press 1986

Kaes, Anton. "*1979* The American television series *Holocaust* is shown in West Germany." *Yale Companion to Jewish Writing and Thought in German Culture, 1096–1996*. New Haven: Yale University Press 1997

Keller, Gottfried. *Sämtliche Werke und Ausgewählte Briefe*. Volume 2. Ed. Clemens Heselhaus. München: Carl Hanser 1963

Kirbach, Roland. "Solingen war die Zäsur." *Die Zeit*, 23 May 1997: 6

Koepnick, Lutz P. "Negotiating Popular Culture: Wenders, Handke, and the Topographies of Cultural Studies." *The German Quarterly* 69, no. 4 (1996): 381–400

Krechel, Rüdiger and Ulrike Reeg, eds. *Werkheft Literatur: Franco Biondi*. München: iudicium 1989

Kristeva, Julia. *Desire in Language: A Semiotic Approach to Literature and Art*. New York: Columbia University Press 1980

Kugelmann, Cilly. "'Tell Them in America We're Still Alive!': The Jewish Community in the Federal Republic." *New German Critique* 46 (1989): 129–40

Kuhn, Anna K. "Bourgeois Ideology and the (Mis)Reading of Günter Wallraff's *Ganz Unten*." *New German Critique* 46 (1989): 191–202

Lappin, Elena, ed. *Jewish Voices – German Words: Growing Up Jewish in Post-war Germany and Austria*. North Haven, Connecticut: Catbird Press 1994

Lauckner, Nancy A. "The Treatment of Problems of Integration in Some Recent Works by Authors from the Former GDR." *Studies in GDR Culture and Society* 14/15. *Changing Identities in East Germany.* Selected Papers from the Nineteenth and Twentieth New Hampshire Symposia, 223–35. Eds. Margy Gerber and Roger Woods. Lanham: University Press of America 1996

Lewis, Derek. "The Role of Language in the Fall of the GDR and the Aftermath." *Germany in the 1990s. German Monitor* 34, 125–34. Ed. H.J. Hahn. Amsterdam: Rodopi 1995

Linke, Uli. "Murderous Fantasies: Violence, Memory, and Selfhood in Germany." *New German Critique* 64 (1995): 37–59

Lionnet, Françoise. *Autobiographical Voices: Race, Gender, Self-Portraiture.* Ithaca: Cornell University Press 1989

Lottman, Joachim. "Kanak Attack!" Interview with Feridun Zaimoglu. *Die Zeit*, 21 November 1997: 24

Markovits, Andrei S. "Rainer Werner Fassbinder's *Garbage, the City and Death*: Renewed Antagonism in the Complex Relationship between Jews and Germans in the Federal Republic of Germany." *New German Critique* 38 (1986): 3–27

Marshall, Jeannie. "Suddenly in Germany, It's Cool to Be Jewish." *Saturday Night*, 29 July 2000. 28–35

Mattson, Michelle. "Refugees in Germany: Invasion or Invention?" *New German Critique* 64 (1995): 61–85

Mede-Flock, Hanne. *Im Schatten der Mondsichel*. Berlin: EXpress Edition 1985

Mohr, Reinhard. *Zaungäste: Die Generation, die nach der Revolte kam.* Frankfurt/Main: Fischer Verlag 1992

Mukherjee, Arun. *Oppositional Aesthetics: Readings from a Hyphenated Space.* Toronto: TSAR Publications 1994

Naoum, Jusuf. "Aus dem Getto heraus." *Eine nicht nur deutsche Literatur: Zur Standortbestimmung der "Ausländerliteratur, 79–81."* Eds. Irmgard Ackermann and Harald Weinrich. München: Piper 1986

Nolden, Thomas. *Junge jüdische Literatur*. Würzburg: Königshausen & Neumann 1995

– "Contemporary German Jewish Literature." *German Life and Letters* 47, no.1 (1994): 77–93

Noll, Chaim. *Leben ohne Deutschland*. Reinbek: Rowohlt Taschenbuch Verlag 1995

– *Nachtgedanken über Deutschland*. Reinbek: Rowohlt Taschenbuch Verlag 1992

Oji, Chima. *Unter die Deutschen gefallen: Erfahrungen eines Afrikaners.* Wuppertal: Peter Hammer 1993

Oliver, José F.A. *Gastling: Lyrik.* Berlin: Das Arabische Buch 1993

– *Weil ich dieses Land liebe: Lyrik.* Berlin: Das Arabische Buch 1991

– *Auf-Bruch: Lyrik.* Berlin: Das Arabische Buch 1989

– *Heimatt und andere Fossile Träume: Lyrik.* Berlin: Das Arabische Buch 1989

Özakin, Aysel. "Ali hinter den Spiegeln." *Literatur Konkret* (1986): 6–9

Özdemir, Cem. *Currywurst und Döner: Integration in Deutschland.* Bergisch Gladbach: Gustav Lübbe Verlag, 1999

Peck, Jeffrey M. "*Methodological Postscript*: What's the Difference? Minority Discourse in German Studies." *New German Critique* 46 (1989): 203–8

Peitsch, Helmut. "Autobiographical Writing as *Vergangenheitsbewältigung* (Mastering the Past)." *German History* 7, no.1 (1989): 47–70

Perkins, William Eric. "the rap attack: an introduction." *Droppin' Science: Critical Essays on Rap Music and Hip Hop Culture.* Ed. William Eric Perkins. Philadelphia: Temple University Press 1996

Pfeiffer, Peter C. "The National Identity of the GDR: Antifascism, Historiography, Literature." *Cultural Transformations in the New Germany: American and German Perspectives*, 23–41. Eds. Friederike Eigler and Peter C. Pfeiffer. Columbia, South Carolina: Camden House 1993

Pichler, Georg. "'Seltsam, daß es mir so wenig ausmacht, nicht anzukommen.' Heimat und Fremde bei Barbara Frischmuth." *Barbara Frischmuth*, 57–72. Ed. Kurt Bartsch. Graz: Literaturverlag Droschl 1992

Pirinçci, Akif. *Yin.* München: Goldmann 1999

– *Der Rumpf.* München: Goldmann 1992

– *Tränen sind immer das Ende: Roman.* München: Goldmann 1991

– *Felidae: Roman.* München: Goldmann 1989

Plenzdorf, Ulrich. *Die neuen Leiden des jungen W.* Frankfurt/Main: Suhrkamp 1992

Pratt, Mary Louise. *Imperial Eyes: Travel Writing and Transculturation.* New York: Routledge 1992

Quinn, Michael. "'Never shoulda been let out the penitentiary': Gangsta Rap and the Struggle over Racial Identity." *Cultural Critique* (1996): 65–89

Räthzel, Nora. "Germany: one race, one nation?" *Race & Class* 32, no. 3 (1990): 31–48

Rampersad, Arnold. "Biography, Autobiography, and Afro-American Culture." *The Yale Review* 73, no. 1 (1983): 1–16

Rathenow, Lutz. "Nachdenken über Deutschland." *Aufbruch in eine andere DDR: Reformer und Oppositionelle zur Zukunft ihres Landes*, 285–93. Ed. Hubertus Knabe. Reinbek: Rowohlt 1990

Reichlin, Igor. "Making a Living – Jews in German Economic Life." *Speaking Out: Jewish Voices from United Germany,* 219–31. Ed. Susan Stern. Berlin: Edition q 1995

Ribbat, Christoph. "Borrowed Beats and Native Tongues: Multicultural Rap in Germany." *German-American Cultural Review* (1997): 14–17

Romero, Christiane Zehl. "Sexual Politics and Christa Wolf's *Was bleibt.*" *Studies in GDR Culture and Society* 11/12. *The End of the GDR and the Problems of Integration.* Selected Papers from the Sixteenth and Seventeenth New Hampshire Symposia on the German Democratic Republic, 157–80. Eds. Margy Gerber and Roger Woods. Lanham: University Press of America 1993

Roth, Joseph. "Juden auf Wanderschaft." *Joseph Roth Werke 2: Das Journalistische Werk 1924–1928,* 827–93. Ed. Klaus Westermann. Köln: Kiepenheuer & Witsch 1990

Salaam ya, Mitume. "The Aesthetics of Rap." *African American Review* 29, no. 2 (1995): 305–15

Said, Edward W. *Orientalism.* New York: Vintage Books 1979

Schiffauer, Werner. *Fremde in der Stadt: Zehn Essays über Kultur und Differenz.* Frankfurt/Main: Suhrkamp 1997

Schneider, Richard Chaim. *Zwischen Welten: Ein jüdisches Leben im heutigen Deutschland.* München: Kindler 1994

Şenocak, Zafer. *Atlas des tropischen Deutschland: Essays.* Berlin: Babel Verlag 1993

Seyhan, Azade. "Lost in Translation: Re-Membering the Mother Tongue in Emine Sevgi Özdamar's *Das Leben ist eine Karawanserei.*" *The German Quarterly* 69, no. 4 (1996): 414–26

Sharpe, Jenny. "Figures of Colonial Resistance." *Modern Fiction Studies* 35, no. 1 (1989): 137–55

Slemon, Stephen. "Unsettling the Empire: Resistance Theory for the Second World." *New Contexts of Canadian Criticism,* 228–40. Eds. Ajay Heble, Donna Palmateer Pennee, and J.R. (Tim) Struthers. Peterborough: Broadview Press 1997

Sommer, Doris. "Resistant Texts and Incompetent Readers." *Poetics Today* 15, no. 4 (1994): 523–51

Spivak, Gayatri. *Outside in the Teaching Machine.* New York: Routledge 1993

Stern, Frank. "The 'Jewish Question' in the 'German Question,' 1945–1990: Reflections in Light of November 9th, 1989." *New German Critique* 52 (1991): 155–72

Stern, Guy. "Barbara Honigmann: A Preliminary Assessment." *Insiders and Outsiders: Jewish and Gentile Culture in Germany and Austria,* 329–

51. Eds. Dagmar C.G. Lorenz and Gabriele Weinberger. Detroit: Wayne State University Press 1994

Suhr, Heidrun. "Ausländerliteratur: Minority Literature in the Federal Republic of Germany." *New German Critique* 46 (1989): 71–103

Tate, Dennis. "Trapped in the Past? The Identity Problems of East German Writers since the *Wende.*" *Germany in the 1990s. German Monitor* 34, 1–16. Ed. H.J. Hahn. Amsterdam: Rodopi 1995

Taufiq, Suleman. "Natürlich Kritik." *Eine nicht nur deutsche Literatur: Zur Standortbestimmung der "Ausländerliteratur,"* 74–8. Eds. Irmgard Ackermann and Harald Weinrich. München: Piper 1986

Teraoka, Arlene Akiko. *East, West, and Others: The Third World in Postwar German Literature.* Lincoln: The University of Nebraska Press 1996

– "*Gastarbeiterliteratur*: The Other Speaks Back." *The Nature and Context of Minority Discourse,* 294–318. Eds. Abdul R. JanMohamed and David Lloyd. Oxford: Oxford University Press 1990

– "Talking 'Turk': On Narrative Strategies and Cultural Stereotypes." *New German Critique* 46 (1989): 104–28

Tiffin, Helen. "Post-Colonial Literatures and Counter-Discourse." *Kunapipi* 9, no. 3 (1987): 17–34

Veteto-Conrad, Marilya. *Finding a Voice: Identity and the Works of German-Language Turkish Writers in the Federal Republic of Germany to 1990.* New York: Peter Lang 1996

Walker, Barbara G. *The Woman's Dictionary of Symbols and Sacred Objects.* San Francisco: HarperCollins 1988

Walker, William. "Satire and Societal Criticism in the GDR Picaresque Novel." *Studies in GDR Culture and Society.* Proceedings of the Sixth International Symposium on the German Democratic Republic, 155–66. Eds. Margy Gerber et al. Washington: University Press of America 1981

Wallraff, Günter. *Ganz Unten: Mit einer Dokumentation der Folgen.* Köln: Kiepenheuer and Witsch 1988

Walwicz, Ania. *Writing.* Melbourne: Rigmarole Books 1982

Weinrich, Harald. "Um eine deutsche Literatur von außen bittend." *Merkur* 37, no. 8 (1983): 911–20

Wierschke, Annette. *Schreiben als Selbstbehauptung: Kulturkonflikt und Identität in den Werken von Aysel Özakin, Alev Tekinay und Emine Sevgi Özdamar.* Frankfurt/Main: Verlag für Interkulturelle Kommunikation 1996

Wolf, Christa. *Was bleibt: Erzählung.* München: Deutscher Taschenbuch Verlag 1994

– *Voraussetzungen einer Erzählung: Kassandra. Frankfurter Poetik-Vorlesungen*
München: Deutscher Taschenbuchverlag 1993

– *Im Dialog: Aktuelle Texte*. Frankfurt/Main: Luchterhand 1990

Woods, Roger. "'Nuancen und Zwischentöne' versus 'muskelprotzende Prosa': Autobiography and the Project of Explaining "How it Was' in the GDR." *Studies in GDR Culture and Society* 14/15. *Changing Identities in East Germany*. Selected Papers from the Nineteenth and Twentieth New Hampshire Symposia, 37–49. Eds. Margy Gerber and Roger Woods. Lanham: University Press of America 1996

Wysling, Hans. "Und immer wieder kehrt Odysseus heim: Das 'Fabelhafte' bei Gottfried Keller." *Gottfried Keller: Elf Essays zu seinem Werk*, 151–62. Ed. Hans Wysling. München: Wilhelm Fink Verlag 1990

Zaimoglu, Feridun. *Koppstoff: Kanak Sprak vom Rande der Gesellschaft*. Hamburg: Rotbuch Verlag 1998

– *Abschaum: Die wahre Geschichte von Ertan Ongun*. Hamburg: Rotbuch Verlag 1997

– *Kanak Sprak: 24 Mißtöne vom Rande der Gesellschaft*. Hamburg: Rotbuch Verlag 1995

Zima, Peter V. "Der Mythos der Monosemie: Parteilichkeit und künstlerischer Standtpunkt." *Literaturwissenschaft und Sozialwissenschaften* 6. *Einführung in Theorie, Geschichte und Funktion der DDR-Literatur*, 77–107. Ed. Hans-Jürgen Schmitt. Stuttgart: Metzler 1975

Zipes, Jack. "The Contemporary German Fascination for Things Jewish: Toward a Jewish Minor Culture." *Reemerging Jewish Culture in Germany: Life and Literature since 1989*, 15–45. Eds. Sander L. Gilman and Karen Remmler. New York: New York University Press 1994

Index